Better Homes and Gardens

Jiffy Cooking

Better Homes and Gardens

Jiffy Cooking

MEREDITH PRESS

New York   Des Moines

© Meredith Corporation, 1967. All Rights Reserved.
Printed in the United States of America.
Fifth Printing, 1969.

CONTENTS

On our cover: Franks with a corkscrew cut are sauced with a tomato soup mixture for Saucy Franks.

Photo at left: Apricot Coconut Ring made from a cake mix and canned fruit has an easygoing Island mood.

Our checked seal assures you that every recipe in Jiffy Cooking is tested and endorsed by the Better Homes and Gardens Test Kitchen. Each recipe is tested until it measures up to the high standards of family appeal, practicality, and downright deliciousness!

MEALS MADE EASY

In today's hurry-up world, a few extra minutes can be precious. When you're hoping to save time for fun and relaxation, hours become priceless. And that's the purpose of this section—to present meal ideas that will give you the time you need. Whether you're a working woman, a busy homemaker, or a bachelor, the ideas assembled here will permit you to serve creative, attractive meals without chaining yourself to the kitchen.

Included you will find menu plans to help with the age-old problem of what to serve. Try substituting other recipes in the menus to suit your family's personal preferences, or use seasonal foods to best advantage. We have included some alternate recipe suggestions, but there are more recipes in the next section which also can be used. In addition to menus for family dinners and lunches, you will find menus for entertaining that will leave you free to be an attentive hostess.

Try to dovetail food preparation activities to make minutes count. For example, cook vegetables in the oven along with a main dish that is baked. You'll find many preparation tips included here to help you save time.

Fix hearty Meat and Potato Pie for the family tonight. It's an idea borrowed from the Cornish pastie but made with a generous measure of convenience—pie crust mix and frozen hash browns. Serve this entree with gently warmed catsup and spiced peaches.

FAMILY DINNERS

MEAT AND POTATO PIE

    2 sticks pie crust mix
    1 pound ground beef
    ½ cup milk
    ½ envelope (¼ cup) *dry* onion
        soup mix
      Dash pepper
      Dash allspice
    1 12-ounce package loose-pack
        frozen hash-brown potatoes,
        thawed

Prepare pie crust mix according to package directions; roll out for 2-crust 9-inch pie. Line 9-inch pie plate with pastry. Combine meat, milk, soup mix, pepper, and allspice; mix gently. Lightly pat into pastry-lined pie plate. Top with potatoes. Adjust top crust; seal and flute edge. Cut design in top pastry. Bake at 350° about 1 hour, or till browned. Serve with warmed catsup. Makes 6 to 8 servings.

CHEESE-TOPPED LETTUCE

      Blue cheese (1 ounce per serving)
      Lettuce, cut in crosswise slices
      Oil and vinegar salad dressing

Thoroughly chill blue cheese in freezer for 20 minutes. Place lettuce slices on salad plates; spoon vinegar and oil dressing over each slice. Shred a generous fluff of cheese over each lettuce slice. Serve immediately.

MENU

Meat and Potato Pie
Spiced Peach
Buttered Broccoli Spears
Cheese-topped Lettuce
Banana Cream Pudding
Coffee   *Milk*

PREPARATION TIPS

For easier rolling out of pastry, use a well-floured pastry cloth and stockinette.

Or, roll pastry between 2 sheets of waxed paper. (Dampen table slightly so paper won't slip.) Peel off top sheet and fit dough, paper side up, into pie plate. Remove paper.

BANANA CREAM PUDDING

    2 3¾- or 3⅝-ounce packages
        instant vanilla pudding mix
    2 cups cold milk
    1 cup dairy sour cream
    ½ teaspoon ground cinnamon
      Dash ground nutmeg
    2 medium bananas, sliced
      Flaked coconut

Combine pudding mix, milk, sour cream, and spices in bowl. Beat till ingredients are well blended. Fold in sliced bananas. Spoon into sherbet glasses; chill till served. Top with coconut before serving. Serves 8.

Duo-dressed Cheese-topped Lettuce is easy and unique. For a fluffy topper, chill the blue cheese well before shredding it.

Baked Bean Pie makes supper preparation a snap. Two favorites—luncheon meat and pork and beans—combine to make a hearty main dish. Accompany with crisp relishes.

BAKED BEAN PIE

  1 12-ounce can luncheon meat
  2 tablespoons maple-flavored syrup

  • • •

  1 1-pound 5-ounce can pork and
     beans in tomato sauce, partially
     drained
  2 tablespoons hot dog relish
  1 teaspoon instant minced onion
  ¼ cup shredded sharp process
     American cheese

Cut luncheon meat in 8 slices; brush each slice with syrup. Arrange meat slices around inner edge of 9-inch pie plate. In saucepan, combine pork and beans, hot dog relish, and onion; bring to boiling. Pour bean mixture into pie plate; sprinkle with shredded cheese. Bake in moderate oven (350°) 20 minutes or till meat is lightly browned. Serves 3 or 4.

PARSLEYED RYE BREAD

Spread 4 slices dark rye bread with about 2 tablespoons softened butter or margarine. Sprinkle with 2 tablespoons snipped parsley. Place on baking sheet and bake in a moderate oven (350°) about 15 minutes, or till toasted. Serve warm. Makes 4 servings.

 **MENU**

Baked Bean Pie
Celery Sticks   *Radish Roses*
<u>or</u> *Tossed Green Salad*
Parsleyed Rye Bread
Peppermint Ice Cream
Coffee   *Milk*

CHERRY CRISP

    1 1-pound 5-ounce can cherry pie
       filling
    ¼ cup coarsely chopped walnuts
    ¼ teaspoon rum extract
    1 package refrigerated crescent
       rolls (8 rolls)
    2 tablespoons butter or margarine,
       melted
    2 tablespoons sugar
       Ground cinnamon

Combine pie filling, nuts, and extract in sauce-pan; heat till bubbling, stirring frequently. Pour into 10x6x1½-inch baking dish.

Unroll refrigerated biscuits and separate in-to triangles. Arrange several triangles over *hot* cherry mixture. (Bake remaining rolls accord-ing to package directions.) Drizzle with melted butter. Sprinkle with sugar; then dash with ground cinnamon. Bake in a moderate oven (375°) for 17 to 20 minutes or till golden brown. Serve warm with ice cream, if desired. Makes 6 to 8 servings.

ORANGE-CHERRY COBBLER

Second time, try peach pie filling—

    1 1-pound 5-ounce can cherry pie
       filling
    ¼ cup water
    1 tablespoon lemon juice
    1 package refrigerated orange
       Danish rolls with icing (8 rolls)

In saucepan, combine pie filling, water, and lemon juice; heat to boiling. Pour into an 8¼x1¾-inch round ovenware cake dish. Top *hot* cherries with rolls, flat side down. Bake in hot oven (400°) 15 to 20 minutes or until rolls are done. Spread tops with the icing that comes in the orange-roll package. Serve warm. Makes 6 to 8 servings.

A robust meal for crisp evenings

← An old-fashioned supper platter features po-tato salad with a new twist. Skillet Potato Salad is sauced with creamy canned soup.

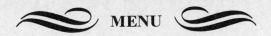

MENU

Bologna Ring
Skillet Potato Salad
Deviled Eggs   Assorted Relishes
Crescent Rolls   Butter
Cherry Crisp or *Orange-cherry Cobbler*
Coffee   Milk

SKILLET POTATO SALAD

    5 slices bacon
    1 10½-ounce can condensed cream
       of celery soup
    2 tablespoons sweet pickle relish
    1 tablespoon instant minced onion
    2 tablespoons vinegar
    ½ teaspoon salt
    1 tablespoon chopped canned pimiento
         • • •
    2 1-pound cans sliced potatoes,
       drained
    1 14-ounce bologna ring

Fry bacon till crisp; remove from skillet; drain and crumble. Drain off bacon fat and return 1 tablespoon to skillet. Blend in soup, relish, onion, vinegar, salt, and pimiento. Cook and stir till mixture comes to boiling.

Gently stir in the sliced potatoes and all but about 1 tablespoon crumbled bacon. Score bologna ring and lay on top of salad in skillet; cover and simmer 10 minutes or till bologna is heated through. Sprinkle remaining bacon over top. Garnish with snipped parsley if de-sired. Serves 6.

DEVILED EGGS

    6 hard-cooked eggs
    ¼ cup mayonnaise or salad dressing
    1 teaspoon vinegar
    1 teaspoon prepared mustard
    ⅛ teaspoon salt
       Dash pepper

Halve eggs lengthwise; remove yolks and mash with pastry blender or fork. Blend in remain-ing ingredients. Refill egg whites. Serves 6.

Cranberry Star Mold has built-in convenience. Serve it the first night with Stuffed Burger Bundles; refrigerate any remaining salad to use with dinner another day.

CRANBERRY STAR MOLD

2 3-ounce packages orange-flavored gelatin
1 1-pound can whole cranberry sauce
• • •
1 8¾-ounce can crushed pineapple, undrained
2 7-ounce bottles ginger ale
Canned orange and grapefruit sections

In saucepan, combine gelatin and cranberry sauce. Heat and stir till almost boiling and gelatin is dissolved. Stir in undrained pineapple and ginger ale. When fizzing has stopped, pour into 5-cup star-shaped mold. Chill till set. Unmold on serving plate.

Garnish with greens and orange and grapefruit sections. If desired, center sections with a few whole cranberries. Serve with mayonnaise or salad dressing. Makes 8 servings.

BLENDER POTS DE CREME

1½ tablespoons unflavored gelatin
2 teaspoons instant coffee powder
½ cup hot milk
1 6-ounce package semi-sweet chocolate pieces
1 tablespoon sugar
½ teaspoon vanilla
2 egg yolks
1¼ cups *drained* finely crushed ice
1 cup whipping cream

Add ¼ cup cold water, gelatin, and coffee to blender container. Cover; blend few seconds on low speed. Add milk; blend till gelatin is dissolved. Add chocolate, sugar, dash salt, and vanilla; cover; blend just till smooth. Add yolks and ice; blend till smooth. While blender is running, add cream. Blend 20 seconds or till it *begins* to thicken. Pour into 5 or 6 small sherbets. Chill 10 minutes. Serves 5 or 6.

PREPARATION TIPS

To unmold gelatin salads, loosen edge with tip of knife. Invert mold on plate. Dip a towel in warm water; wring out; lay on top of mold for few seconds. Lift off the mold.

Or, loosen edge of mold and dip mold just to rim in warm water for few seconds. Tilt mold slightly; ease gelatin to let air in. Tilt and rotate mold so air can loosen it. Put plate over mold; invert; lift off mold.

If serving plate is slightly wet, gelatin can be positioned on plate after removing mold.

STUFFED BURGER BUNDLES

1 cup herb-seasoned stuffing mix
⅓ cup evaporated milk
1 pound ground beef
1 10½-ounce can condensed cream of mushroom soup
2 teaspoons Worcestershire sauce
1 tablespoon catsup

Prepare stuffing according to package directions. Combine evaporated milk and meat; divide in 5 patties. On waxed paper, pat each to 6-inch circle. Put ¼ cup stuffing in center of each; draw meat over stuffing; seal. Place in 1½-quart casserole. Combine remaining ingredients; heat; pour over meat. Bake, uncovered, at 350° for 45 minutes. Serves 5.

HOT DEVILED POTATOES

Packaged instant mashed potatoes (enough for 4 servings)
½ cup dairy sour cream
2 teaspoons prepared mustard
½ teaspoon sugar
2 tablespoons chopped green onion

Prepare potatoes according to package directions. Heat sour cream (do not boil). Add mustard, ½ teaspoon salt, and sugar; stir to blend. Mix into hot potatoes with onion. Immediately turn into 1-quart casserole. Sprinkle with paprika, if desired. Heat in a 350° oven about 10 minutes. Makes 5 servings.

Just wrap ground beef around prepared stuffing mix; top with pepped-up canned soup for easy Stuffed Burger Bundles.

LEMON SAUCED CAKE

1 cup cold milk
¾ cup light corn syrup
1 3¾-ounce package *instant* lemon pudding mix
½ cup broken pecans
2 teaspoons lemon juice
Pound cake slices

Stir milk and corn syrup into pudding mix. Beat thoroughly. Stir in nuts and lemon juice. Serve over pound cake. Makes 2 cups.

 **MENU**

Stuffed Burger Bundles
Hot Deviled Potatoes <u>or</u> *Mashed Potatoes*
Green Beans
Cranberry Star Mold
Lemon Sauced Cake <u>or</u> *Blender Pots De Creme*
Coffee   Milk

When minutes count, serve Saucy Corned Beef Burgers with mashed potatoes whipped up from a packaged instant product. While burgers bake, prepare salad and a dessert.

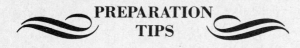

PREPARATION TIPS

When chopping onion or green pepper for a recipe, chop an extra supply, then freeze the surplus for use later.

Clean salad greens as soon as possible after bringing home from the market. Drain greens thoroughly on paper toweling as other groceries are being put away. Store greens in clear plastic bags in the refrigerator.

Use kitchen shears to snip parsley.

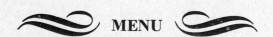

MENU

Saucy Corned Beef Burgers
Mashed Potatoes
Basil Carrots or *Green Beans with Bacon*
Lettuce Wedges   Salad Dressing
Frosty Green Grapes
Coffee   Milk

SAUCY CORNED BEEF BURGERS

1 12-ounce can corned beef, finely chopped
½ cup mayonnaise or salad dressing
2 tablespoons instant minced onion
1 teaspoon prepared horseradish
   Dash pepper
1 beaten egg
1 tablespoon water
½ cup fine dry bread crumbs
2 tablespoons shortening
3 slices sharp process American cheese
1 8¼-ounce can mixed vegetables
1 10½-ounce can condensed cream of mushroom soup
⅓ cup milk

Combine corned beef, mayonnaise, onion, horseradish, and pepper; shape into 6 patties. Blend egg and water; dip patties into egg, then crumbs. Brown lightly in hot shortening. Place patties in 10x6x1½-inch baking dish. Quarter cheese slices diagonally; overlap 2 triangles atop each patty. Drain vegetables. Combine with soup and milk; heat. Pour over patties. Bake at 350° for 12 minutes. Serves 6.

BASIL CARROTS

> 2 tablespoons butter or margarine
> 6 medium carrots, thinly sliced
> on the bias
> ¼ teaspoon salt
> ¼ teaspoon dried basil, crushed

In medium skillet, melt the butter or margarine; add the sliced carrots. Sprinkle with salt and basil. Cover skillet and simmer 10 to 12 minutes, or just till carrots are tender. Garnish with parsley. Makes 6 servings.

GREEN BEANS WITH BACON

Soy sauce adds an oriental touch to canned green beans—

> 4 slices bacon
> ¼ cup finely chopped onion
> 1 clove garlic, minced
> 2 tablespoons soy sauce
> 2 1-pound cans cut green beans,
> well drained

Cook bacon till crisp; drain, reserving 2 tablespoons fat. Crumble bacon.

Cook onion and garlic in reserved fat till tender. Stir in soy sauce; add beans. Cook, stirring frequently, till hot. Just before serving, stir in bacon. Makes 6 servings.

These Basil Carrots are subtly herbed to enhance the carrot flavor. Or, substitute Beans with Bacon to round out the meal.

If desired, a sprinkling of creme de cacao over individual servings of Frosty Green Grapes will make an extra elegant topper.

FROSTY GREEN GRAPES

> 3 cups seedless green
> grapes, chilled
> ½ cup dairy sour cream
> Brown sugar

Wash, stem, and drain grapes thoroughly. Just before serving, add sour cream; mix carefully, coating grapes well. Spoon into dishes; top with sugar. Serves 6.

JUBILEE SAUCE

Thoroughly combine one 16-ounce jar (1⅓ cups) dark cherry preserves with ¼ cup port wine and ¼ teaspoon almond extract in a small bowl; chill. Serve over vanilla ice cream. Makes 1⅔ cups sauce.

MANDARIN FIG WHIP

Prepare one 2-ounce package dessert topping mix according to package directions. Blend in one 8-ounce carton orange yogurt. Fold in one 11-ounce can mandarin oranges, drained, 1 cup diced fig-filled cookies, and ¼ cup coarsely chopped walnuts.

Chill at least 3 to 4 hours. Stir just before serving to fluff up mixture. Pile lightly into sherbet glasses. Makes 6 servings.

CANADIAN BACON STACK-UPS

Meat and potatoes all bake together—

- 1 cup whole cranberry sauce
- 2 tablespoons light corn syrup
- 1 1-pound 1-ounce can sweet potatoes, drained
- 1 tablespoon butter or margarine, melted
- 1 tablespoon brown sugar
- ¼ teaspoon ground ginger
- 1 pound unsliced Canadian-style bacon

Combine the cranberry sauce and light corn syrup in a bowl.

With an electric mixer, beat potatoes with butter, brown sugar, and ginger till light and fluffy. Slice bacon into 12 pieces. In 10x6x1½-inch baking dish spread *half* of the potato mixture equally on *half* of the bacon slices. Cover with remaining 6 bacon slices and top each with a mound of potatoes. Drizzle cranberry sauce over stacks. Bake in a moderate oven (350°) for 15 minutes, basting once or twice with sauce in dish. Serves 6.

PREPARATION TIPS

To make Carrot Curls, first pare carrots. Cut thin lengthwise strips with vegetable parer. (Rest carrot on board; pare away from you.) Roll up long slices; use wooden pick to hold. Chill in ice water. Remove picks to serve.

If short on time, make Carrot Crisps. Using parer, slice pared carrots crosswise. Chill thin circles in ice water—they'll ruffle.

To make Celery Fans, cut celery stalks in 3- or 4-inch lengths. Make parallel cuts close together from one end almost to other. Or slit both ends of celery stalks almost to center. Chill in ice water till strips curl.

Fit for the king of the household

← Canadian Bacon Stack-ups served with crisp relishes and asparagus spears make a picture-pretty dinner for the hungry family.

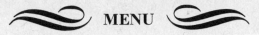

MENU

Canadian Bacon Stack-ups
Asparagus Spears <u>or</u> Green Beans Amandine
Lime Applesauce Mold   Crisp Relishes
Crescent Rolls   Butter
Brownie Treats
Coffee   Milk

LIME APPLESAUCE MOLD

- 1 1-pound can applesauce
- 1 3-ounce package lime-flavored gelatin
- 1 7-ounce bottle lemon-lime carbonated beverage (about 1 cup)

MAKE AHEAD RECIPE

Combine applesauce and gelatin in saucepan. Cook and stir till gelatin dissolves. Gently stir in carbonated beverage. Turn into a 3-cup mold. Chill till firm. Serves 6.

GREEN BEANS AMANDINE

- 3 tablespoons slivered almonds
- 3 tablespoons butter or margarine
- 2 9-ounce packages frozen French-style green beans

In skillet, lightly brown almonds in butter. Stir occasionally. Meanwhile, cook beans according to package directions; drain. Pour almond mixture over beans. Serves 6.

BROWNIE TREATS

- 1 1-pound package brownie mix
- ½ 1-pint jar marshmallow creme
- 2 tablespoons green creme de menthe
  Vanilla ice cream

Prepare fudge-type brownies according to package directions. Cool slightly; cut into large bars or squares. Blend together the marshmallow creme and creme de menthe. To serve, top each brownie with a scoop of ice cream. Spoon mint sauce over top. Serves 6.

COMPANY OCCASIONS

MENU

Fruit Cup
Pampered Beef Filets
with Royal Mushroom Sauce
Carrots Piquant
Buttered Peas and Onions
Cloverleaf Rolls   Butter
Quick Fudge Sundaes
Demitasse

PAMPERED BEEF FILETS

    6 large mushrooms
    2 tablespoons butter or margarine
    6 beef filets
       Royal Mushroom Sauce

Trim and chip-carve mushroom crowns.* (The chopped stems will be used in sauce.) Heat butter in heavy skillet till golden brown and bubbling. Quickly brown steaks on both sides over moderately high heat. Place filets on squares of heavy foil on baking sheet.

Spoon 2 tablespoons Royal Mushroom Sauce over each filet; top each with a mushroom crown. Bring corners of each foil square up over steak and twist gently, leaving top slightly open. Complete cooking in extremely hot oven (500°) 12 minutes for rare, 15 minutes for medium, and 18 minutes for well done. (Or, refrigerate meat before finishing off in oven and allow the chilly steaks to cook 10 minutes longer.) Makes 6 servings.

*Holding sharp paring knife on slant, cut V-shaped piece out of center tops of mushrooms. Make second cut at right angle to first.

Treat your dinner guests elegantly

← Pampered Beef Filets with Royal Mushroom Sauce are browned, crowned with mushrooms, and wrapped in foil for easy cooking.

ROYAL MUSHROOM SAUCE

Add ½ cup chopped fresh mushroom stems and ¼ cup finely chopped green onions to fat remaining in skillet after filets have been browned. Cook till tender, but not brown. Blend 4 teaspoons cornstarch with ½ cup cold water. Add to skillet with 1 cup burgundy, 2 tablespoons snipped parsley, 1 teaspoon salt, and dash pepper. Cook and stir till mixture thickens. At serving time, reheat remaining sauce and pass during meal. Makes 1½ cups.

CARROTS PIQUANT

    2 1-pound cans (4 cups) small
       whole carrots
    1 tablespoon cornstarch
    ¼ teaspoon salt
       Several dashes nutmeg
    ⅔ cup orange juice
    2 tablespoons butter or margarine
       Snipped parsley

Drain carrots, reserving ¼ cup liquid. In saucepan, blend cornstarch with salt and nutmeg; stir in the reserved carrot liquid and orange juice. Cook, stirring constantly, till mixture thickens and boils. Boil 2 minutes, stirring constantly.

Add butter or margarine and carrots; heat through. Sprinkle with parsley before serving. Makes 6 to 8 servings.

QUICK FUDGE SUNDAES

    1 6-ounce package (1 cup)
       semisweet chocolate pieces
    1 6-ounce can evaporated milk
    ½ 1-pint jar marshmallow creme
       Vanilla ice cream

Combine chocolate pieces and milk in a saucepan; heat slowly, stirring till blended. Beat in marshmallow creme till blended. Serve warm or cool over vanilla ice cream. Makes 2 cups.

20

PREPARATION TIPS

Before browning the chops, prepare beans by placing two 10-ounce packages frozen Italian green beans in a shallow baking dish. Add a little butter, salt, and pepper. Cover. Put them in the oven when you start browning the chops. They'll be done when the chops are.

Fill the coffee maker, ready for plugging in as dinner goes on the table.

At the last minute, pop rolls into the oven to heat quickly.

Pour the Hot Sherried Consomme into warmed goblets at the table. To prevent goblets from cracking, put a teaspoon in the goblet. It will absorb some of the heat.

Kitchen shears make a quick job of snipping candied ginger for Gingered Pineapple.

PORK CHOPS ON AMBER RICE

The tangy flavor of orange juice sparks this pork chop and rice combination—

    6 pork chops, ¾-inch thick
      Salt and pepper
 1⅓ cups packaged precooked rice
    1 cup orange juice
    1 10½-ounce can condensed chicken-
      rice soup

Brown pork chops in heavy skillet; season with salt and pepper. Place rice in 12x7½x2-inch baking dish; pour orange juice over rice. Arrange browned pork chops on rice. Pour chicken soup over all. Cover; bake in moderate oven (350°) for 45 minutes. Uncover and bake 10 minutes longer. Makes 6 servings.

When time is of the essence, count on this meal featuring Pork Chops on Amber Rice to be a success. The main dish can be put in the oven and almost forgotten till served.

MENU

Hot Sherried Consomme   Saltines
Pork Chops on Amber Rice
Buttered Italian Green Beans
Lettuce Wedges   Zippy Beet Dressing
Hot Rolls   Butter
Gingered Pineapple
Coffee   Milk

HOT SHERRIED CONSOMME

In saucepan, heat two 10½-ounce cans condensed consomme, 1⅓ cups water, and 6 tablespoons dry sherry. Transfer to warmed server. Pour over thin lemon or lime slices in warmed goblets at table after guests are seated. Serve with saltines. Serves 6.

ZIPPY BEET DRESSING

    1 8-ounce can (1 cup) diced beets
    ½ cup mayonnaise or salad dressing
    1½ teaspoons prepared horseradish
       Dash salt
    1 medium head lettuce

Thoroughly drain beets, reserving liquid. Mash beets slightly with fork; stir in mayonnaise, horseradish, and dash salt. Add beet juice if needed to make mixture of desired consistency. Chill if desired. Core lettuce and cut in 6 wedges. Spoon on beet dressing. Makes 6 servings.

GINGERED PINEAPPLE

    1 cup dairy sour cream
    ¼ cup honey
    2 tablespoons snipped
       candied ginger
    1 1-pound 4½-ounce can pineapple
       chunks, chilled and drained (2 cups)

MAKE AHEAD RECIPE

Combine first 3 ingredients; chill. To serve, spoon over drained pineapple in individual serving dishes. Makes 6 servings.

Salad and Dessert Dress Ups

A combination of beets, mayonnaise, and horseradish in Zippy Beet Dressing makes a pretty deep pink dressing with robust flavor.

Candied ginger perks up canned pineapple, while honey adds a subtle sweetness to this refreshing dessert—Gingered Pineapple.

PEPPY SALAD DRESSING

1 cup chilled French dressing
½ cup dairy sour cream
½ cup finely chopped green pepper
Dash chili powder

Combine all ingredients till blended. Serve over a mixed tossed vegetable salad. Makes about 1¾ cups dressing.

ONION FRENCH DRESSING

1 cup clear French dressing
  with herbs and spices
1 teaspoon Worcestershire
  sauce
2 tablespoons thinly sliced
  green onion

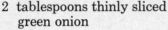

In a small jar, combine all ingredients. Chill several hours. Shake vigorously just before serving. Serve over a mixed tossed vegetable salad. Makes about 1 cup dressing.

WINE SPICED PEACHES

1 1-pound 13-ounce can peach halves
2 tablespoons sugar
2 3-inch cinnamon sticks,
  broken in halves
2 tablespoons orange juice
½ cup sauterne

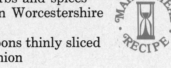

Drain peaches, reserving ⅔ cup syrup. Combine syrup with sugar and cinnamon pieces in saucepan. Bring to boiling and boil 5 minutes. Remove from heat. Blend in orange juice and wine. Pour over peaches in bowl. Chill overnight. Serve with macaroon cookies and vanilla ice cream if desired. Serves 4 to 6.

PREPARATION TIPS

Bake the main dish and refrigerated butter-layered loaves side-by-side in the same oven.

For ease of preparation and storage of salad dressings with vinegar and oil base, combine ingredients in a jar with a tight-fitting cover. The ingredients can be thoroughly shaken, stored, and served in the same container.

MENU

Seafood Bake
Buttered Broccoli Spears
Tossed Vegetable Salad
Peppy Salad Dressing or
Onion French Dressing
Butter-layered Loaves   Butter
Wine Spiced Peaches   Macaroon Cookies
Coffee   Milk

SEAFOOD BAKE

1 10½-ounce can condensed cream
  of celery soup
¼ cup milk
1 beaten egg
¼ cup grated Parmesan cheese
    • • •
1 7½-ounce can crab meat, drained,
  flaked, and cartilage removed
1 4½-ounce can shrimp, drained
1 3-ounce can sliced mushrooms,
  drained
    • • •
3 tablespoons fine dry bread crumbs
1 tablespoon butter or margarine,
  melted

Combine cream of celery soup, milk, egg, and *half* the cheese in a saucepan. Stir over low heat till cheese is melted and mixture is hot. Stir in crab, shrimp, and mushrooms. Spoon into 4 large baking shells.

Toss dry bread crumbs with remaining 2 tablespoons cheese and melted butter. Sprinkle crumbs over mixture in shells.

Bake in a moderate oven (375°) about 20 minutes. Garnish with parsley and lemon twist. Makes 4 servings.

A breeze of a meal to make

Seafood Bake with lemon twists and Wine →
Spiced Peaches are highlights of this company dinner. Serve with a white wine.

MENU

Corn Chips   Dip a la Spaghetti
Tamale Hero Sandwiches
or
Tuna Burgers
Party Potato Chips   Zippy Almonds
Dill Pickle-sickles
Ice Cream Cups   Cookies
Cider

TAMALE HERO SANDWICHES

    3 hero buns
    ¼ cup chopped green pepper
    1 tablespoon instant minced onion
    1 15-ounce can chili with beans
    1 15-ounce can tamales
    3 ounces sharp natural Cheddar
       cheese, shredded (¾ cup)

Slice hero buns in half lengthwise and toast.
Add green pepper and onion to chili; spread
buns with chili mixture. Split tamales lengthwise and arrange atop chili. Sprinkle with
shredded cheese. Place under broiler for about
10 minutes or till cheese melts and sandwiches
are heated. Makes 6 open-face sandwiches.

TUNA BURGERS

    1 6-ounce can evaporated milk
    3 slices white bread with crusts
       removed
    ½ envelope French salad dressing
       mix
    2 6½- or 7-ounce cans tuna, drained
    4 hamburger buns, split

Pour milk over bread in mixing bowl; add salad dressing mix. Stir with fork till well blended. Stir in tuna. Spoon tuna mixture onto 8
hamburger bun halves. Place sandwiches under broiler 6 inches from heat; broil 4 minutes
or till tuna is lightly browned and heated
through. If desired, garnish with olive slices.
Makes 8 open-face sandwiches.

DIP A LA SPAGHETTI

Stir 1 tablespoon dry spaghetti sauce mix into 1 cup dairy sour cream with 1 tablespoon
finely chopped green pepper. Chill. Serve as
dip for crisp vegetables or corn chips.

PARTY POTATO CHIPS

    1 4-ounce package potato
       chips (about 7 cups)
    2 ounces process American
       cheese, shredded (½ cup)
       Dried thyme, basil, or marjoram,
       crushed

Spread potato chips on baking sheet and
sprinkle with cheese. Sprinkle lightly with
thyme, basil, or marjoram. Heat at 350° for 5
minutes or till cheese melts. Serve hot.

ZIPPY ALMONDS

    ¼ cup butter or margarine
    ¼ cup salad oil
    1½ cups blanched whole almonds
       (about ½ pound)
    1 tablespoon celery salt
    ½ teaspoon salt
    ⅛ teaspoon cayenne

Combine butter, oil, and almonds in heavy
skillet. Stir frequently over medium heat till
almonds are golden brown. Remove almonds
from oil; drain. Mix seasonings and sprinkle
over hot nuts, stirring to coat.

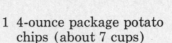

ICE CREAM CUPS

Fill waffle cuplets with 2 scoops of chocolate
ice cream. Drizzle with Chocolate Topping:
Melt ½ cup semisweet chocolate pieces with 4
tablespoons butter over hot water. Sprinkle
with chopped pecans. Freeze till firm.

An informal teen-age record party

Teen-agers will devour the Tamale Hero →
Sandwiches, hot from the oven. What better
partners than corn chips and pickle-sickles.

Plan sandwiches hot off the griddle for a make-it-yourself buffet. Along with Boston Beanwiches and Ham 'n Cheese Sandwiches, grill pineapple rings till lightly browned.

BOSTON BEANWICH

Butter one side of a whole wheat bread slice. Turn over and spread with ¼ cup drained, canned baked beans in molasses sauce. Crumble 2 slices crisp-cooked bacon over beans. Top with slice of sharp process American cheese.

Spread second slice of bread with prepared mustard and add atop, mustard side down. Butter the top of sandwich.

Grill both sides till baked beans are hot through and cheese melts slightly. Serve with sweet pickles. Makes 1 serving.

HAM 'N CHEESE SANDWICH

To make sandwich, spread slice of rye bread with sharp cheese spread and another slice with deviled ham from a can. Put sandwich together; butter top and bottom. Grill both sides till toasted. Garnish with pimiento-stuffed olive on wooden pick. Makes 1 serving.

GRILLED CHEESE ITALIANO

Top a slice of Italian bread with a slice each of mozzarella cheese and salami. Dash on crushed oregano. Top with second bread slice.

Generously butter top and bottom of sandwich. Grill on both sides. Anchor with a cherry pepper speared on wooden pick. Complement with corn chips. Makes 1 serving.

GERMAN HAM-SWISSER

Mix ¼ cup softened butter or margarine with 2 tablespoons prepared horseradish-mustard, 2 tablespoons finely chopped onion, and 2 teaspoons poppy seed; spread on 4 slices rye bread.

Top each with thin slice of boiled ham, slice of Swiss cheese, then slice of rye bread. Butter tops and bottoms of sandwiches. Grill on both sides till hot and cheese melts. Pass extra poppy-seed butter. Serves 4.

STEAK SANDWICH WITH SAUCE

- ½ cup butter or margarine
- 3 tablespoons bottled steak sauce
- 2 tablespoons sliced green onion
- 1½ tablespoons Worcestershire sauce
- ¼ teaspoon salt
  Instant meat tenderizer
- 1 pound (¼ inch thick) round steak, cut in 6 pieces
- 6 slices (1 inch thick) French bread, toasted

Melt butter; add steak sauce, onion, Worcestershire, and salt; heat. Use instant meat tenderizer on round steak according to label directions. Preheat grill according to the manufacturer's directions; grease grill lightly. Grill meat 2 to 3 minutes per side. Sprinkle with pepper. To serve, dip slice of toast quickly in hot butter sauce; top with steak. Spoon on remaining sauce. Makes 6 sandwiches.

JAVA ANGEL CAKE

- 1 package angel cake mix
- 1 tablespoon instant coffee powder
- 1 teaspoon vanilla
  Mocha Topping

Prepare cake mix according to package directions, *but dissolve instant coffee in the water.* Add vanilla. Bake cake as directed on package. Cool thoroughly.

Spread with *Mocha Topping:* Combine 1½ cups whipping cream, 3 tablespoons sugar, 2 tablespoons cocoa (regular-type, dry), 2 teaspoons instant coffee powder, and ¾ teaspoon vanilla. Whip till fluffy. Spread on cake; chill.

MENU

Assorted Grilled Sandwiches
Grilled Pineapple Rings
Potato Chips
Pickles   Olives   Celery Sticks
Orange-cream Dessert <u>or</u> *Java Angel Cake*
Coffee   Milk

The perfect end to the sandwich buffet is delicately flavored Orange-cream Dessert. Accompany with mugs of piping-hot coffee.

ORANGE-CREAM DESSERT

Sour cream in the frosting gives an unusual tang and a good spreading consistency. Use a spatula to swirl on the frosting—

- 1 teaspoon shredded orange peel
- ½ cup orange juice
- ½ cup sugar
- 1 cup orange juice

• • •

- 1 baked 10-inch sponge cake
- 1 cup whipping cream
- ¼ cup sugar
- 1 teaspoon shredded orange peel
- 1 cup dairy sour cream

Combine 1 teaspoon peel, ½ cup orange juice, and ½ cup sugar. Heat and stir till sugar dissolves. Add 1 cup orange juice; cool. Drizzle over top, bottom, and sides of cake.

Combine whipping cream with ¼ cup sugar and 1 teaspoon orange peel; beat till stiff peaks form. Fold in sour cream till blended. Spread evenly over top and sides of cake. Chill several hours. Makes 10 to 12 servings.

Deviled Ham Pie rates high as a luncheon dish. Deviled ham is surrounded with pastry, then topped with asparagus spears. Prepare easy cheese sauce from canned soup.

DEVILED HAM PIE

Prepare 1 stick pie crust mix according to package directions. Divide in half. Roll out one half on lightly floured surface to 7-inch circle. Trim with pastry wheel or knife. Place on ungreased baking sheet.

Spread with one 4½-ounce can deviled ham to within ½ inch of edge. Top with one 3-ounce can chopped mushrooms, drained (½ cup). Roll remaining pastry to 7-inch circle; trim. Place over filling; crimp edges together. Prick top with fork.

Bake in a hot oven (425°) for 15 minutes or till lightly browned.

Cook one 10-ounce package frozen asparagus spears according to package directions, omitting the salt from cooking water. Drain.

Combine one 11-ounce can condensed Cheddar cheese soup and ¼ cup milk in a small saucepan. Heat. Transfer pie to plate. Arrange asparagus spears on top in spoke fashion. Cut in wedges and top with the cheese sauce. Makes 4 servings.

 **MENU**

Deviled Ham Pie
Tomato Slices on Lettuce
Pickles   Olives
Cantaloupe a la Mode
Coffee   Tea

LAZY DAY GRASSHOPPER PIE

A dessert that can be made the night before and forgotten till serving time—

Chocolate wafer cookies
1 1-pint jar marshmallow creme
¼ cup milk
4 drops peppermint extract
6 or 7 drops green food coloring
• • •
1 cup whipping cream, whipped

Line bottom of 9-inch pie plate with chocolate wafer cookies, filling in spaces between with pieces of cookie. Line sides of the pie plate with half-cookies.

In mixing bowl, combine marshmallow creme, milk, peppermint extract, and food coloring; whip till fluffy. Fold in whipped cream. Spoon filling into cookie crust. Freeze till firm, 8 hours or overnight. Garnish with dollops of additional whipped cream, if desired. Makes 6 to 8 servings.

EASY APRICOT SOUFFLE

A glamorous dessert that takes only minutes to prepare and only one bowl for preparation and chilling. Tastes divine, too—

2 packages vanilla whipped dessert mix
1 12-ounce can (1½ cups) apricot nectar, chilled
1 cup canned apricot pie filling

In a deep, narrow bowl (about the size of the small bowl of an electric mixer), thoroughly blend dessert mix and 1 *cup* of the apricot nectar. Whip at highest speed of electric mixer for 1 minute. Add remaining apricot nectar; whip at highest speed of electric mixer 2 minutes longer.

With kitchen shears, snip through apricots in the apricot pie filling. Fold into the whipped mixture; smooth top. Chill in mixing bowl till set, about 2 to 3 hours.

Unmold on dessert platter. Garnish with pressurized whipped cream and small whole canned apricots or additional apricot pie filling. Makes 6 to 8 servings.

TURKEY AMANDINE ON TOAST

2 10¾-ounce cans chicken gravy
2 cups cubed cooked turkey* or chicken
2 tablespoons chopped canned pimiento
⅛ teaspoon poultry seasoning
1 cup dairy sour cream
2 tablespoons all-purpose flour
½ cup slivered almonds
Toast points

Combine gravy, turkey, pimiento, and poultry seasoning in a saucepan. Heat; stir occasionally. Combine sour cream and flour; stir into turkey mixture and heat just to boiling. Add almonds and serve over toast points. Garnish with parsley. Makes 6 to 8 servings.

*Use leftover cooked turkey or chicken or a cooked boneless turkey roast.

CRANBERRY RELISH SQUARES

A gelatin salad that's made in just one step. No need to chill before adding fruit—

2 3-ounce packages raspberry-flavored gelatin
2 cups boiling water
2 10-ounce packages frozen cranberry-orange relish
1 7-ounce bottle lemon-lime carbonated beverage

Dissolve gelatin in boiling water. Stir in the frozen relish till melted. Carefully stir in the carbonated beverage. Pour into 8x8x2-inch pan. Chill till firm. Cut in squares. Serve on lettuce. Makes 6 to 8 servings.

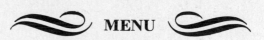

MENU

Turkey Amandine on Toast
French-style Green Beans
Cranberry Relish Squares
Celery Sticks
Lazy Day Grasshopper Pie or
Easy Apricot Souffle
Coffee   Tea

MENU

Broiled Grapefruit
Waffles with Toppers   *Sausage*
Coffee   *Milk*

WAFFLES WITH TOPPERS

Prepare desired amount of packaged pancake mix according to package directions for waffles.

In small bowl, combine 2 tablespoons flaked coconut and 1 tablespoon shredded orange peel. In another bowl, combine ¼ cup diced unpared apple, 1 teaspoon sugar, and several dashes ground nutmeg. Have ¼ cup chopped pecans ready. Pour batter onto preheated waffle baker; *quickly* top with a small amount of your choice of fruit mixtures or pecans. Bake. Serve with butter, syrup, and sausage.

SHRIMP DEVILED EGGS

Substitute this dish with toasted English muffins for the waffles and sausage—

- 8 hard-cooked eggs
- ⅓ cup Thousand Island dressing
- 3 tablespoons all-purpose flour
- 1 10-ounce can frozen condensed cream of shrimp soup, thawed
- 1 cup milk
- ½ cup shredded sharp Cheddar cheese
- ⅓ cup buttered bread crumbs

Halve eggs lengthwise. Remove yolks; mash; combine with dressing. Pile into whites. Arrange in 10x6x1½-inch baking dish. Blend flour and soup; stir in milk. Cook and stir till mixture boils. Stir in cheese till melted; pour over eggs. Sprinkle crumbs over all. Bake at 350° for 15 to 20 minutes. Serves 6.

Perfect for an easy Sunday brunch

← Dress up an everyday mix for company by serving golden Waffles with Toppers. Accompany them with browned sausage links.

BROILED GRAPEFRUIT

- 3 grapefruit
  Butter or margarine
- 3 tablespoons sugar
- ¾ teaspoon ground cinnamon
  Stemmed maraschino cherries

Have grapefruit at room temperature. Cut each in half; then cut a thin slice from the bottom of each half to balance grapefruit. Cut around every section, close to the membrane—fruit should be completely loosened from shell. Remove core from each half; dot with butter or margarine.

Combine the sugar and cinnamon; sprinkle over grapefruit halves. Place on broiler rack or in shallow baking pan; broil 4 inches from heat about 8 minutes or till heated through and bubbling. Garnish with stemmed maraschino cherries. Makes 6 servings.

ELEGANT GRAPEFRUIT

MAKE AHEAD RECIPE

Prepare Broiled Grapefruit above, except omit dotting with butter, sugar, and spice.

Combine 6 tablespoons melted butter, 6 tablespoons orange liqueur, and 1 tablespoon sugar; drizzle over cut fruit. Let stand at room temperature about 2 hours to marinate fruit. Broil as above or till tops of fruit are brown and bubbling hot. Makes 6 servings.

Broiled Grapefruit is served bubbling hot as the right beginning to a brunch. Stemmed maraschino cherries give it a party flair.

TROPIC ISLE APPETIZER

1½ cups unsweetened pineapple
juice, chilled
½ cup orange juice, chilled
2 drops aromatic bitters

• • •

1 7-ounce bottle ginger ale,
chilled (about 1 cup)
½ pint pineapple sherbet

Combine chilled pineapple juice and orange juice; add aromatic bitters. Divide among 4 chilled glasses. Tip each glass and pour ginger ale down side to fill. Top each serving with a scoop of pineapple sherbet. If desired, thread fresh fruit (strawberries, melon balls) on glass straws for kabob stirrers. Garnish with a sprig of fresh mint. Makes 4 servings.

QUICK CHICKEN VERONIQUE

Almost as simple as opening two cans—

2 10½-ounce cans chicken a la king
¼ cup dry white wine
1 tablespoon butter or margarine
1 8-ounce can seedless green
grapes, drained (1 cup)

• • •

Cooked rice (enough for 4 servings)
Toasted slivered almonds*

Combine chicken a la king, wine, butter, and grapes. Heat thoroughly. Serve over hot cooked rice; garnish with toasted slivered almonds. Makes 4 servings.

*Toast slivered almonds in shallow baking pan in a moderate oven (350°) for 10 minutes or till golden; stir occasionally. Store remainder in covered container in refrigerator for future use in other recipes.

MENU

Tropic Isle Appetizer or Tomato Juice
Quick Chicken Veronique   Rice
Asparagus Spears
Coffee   Tea

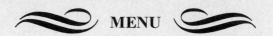

MENU

Canadian-style Bacon
Orange-nut Ring   Butter
Berry-cereal Parfaits
Coffee   Tea

BERRY-CEREAL PARFAITS

1 quart vanilla ice cream
2 10-ounce packages frozen sliced
strawberries, partially thawed
2 cups sugar-frosted corn flakes

In each tall parfait glass, layer about ¼ cup vanilla ice cream, about 3 tablespoons partially thawed strawberries, and ¼ cup corn flakes. Top with another ¼ cup vanilla ice cream and garnish with fresh strawberry halves, if desired. Makes 8 servings.

ORANGE-NUT RING

2 packages refrigerated orange or
cinnamon Danish rolls with
icing (16 rolls)
¼ cup chopped pecans

Separate rolls and arrange 1 package (8 rolls), flat side down, around bottom of ungreased 6½-cup ring mold. Stagger remaining package of rolls on top of first layer, covering seams of rolls on bottom layer.

Bake at 375° for 20 to 25 minutes. Invert on serving plate while warm. Spread top and sides with frosting included in packages. Decorate with nuts. Serve warm with butter. Makes 8 servings.

Serve with sliced Canadian-style bacon browned lightly in a skillet.

A light brunch for the ladies

Simply make the Orange-nut Ring from re- ➡
frigerated rolls; serve with colorful Berry-cereal Parfaits and Canadian-style bacon.

EVERYDAY LUNCHES

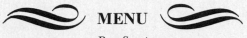

MENU

Pea Soup
Toasted Swiss Sandwiches
Carrot Curls   *Radish Roses*
Choco-mint Fluff   *Angel Cake*
Milk

CHOCO-MINT FLUFF

Combine 1 cup whipping cream, ½ cup pre-sweetened instant cocoa powder, and 2 drops peppermint flavoring; chill. Whip to soft peaks. Serve on angel cake slices; top with crushed peppermint candy. Makes 1½ cups.

TOASTED SWISS SANDWICHES

Poppy seed and onion butter give grilled cheese sandwiches new zest—

- 4 slices Swiss cheese
- 8 slices white bread
- 2 teaspoons poppy seed

  • • •

- 1 teaspoon minced onion
- ¼ cup butter or margarine

Place a slice of cheese on *four slices* of bread. Sprinkle each slice of cheese with ½ teaspoon poppy seed. Top each slice of cheese with remaining four bread slices. Combine the onion with butter. Spread on top and bottom of sandwiches. Grill both sides till golden brown. Makes 4 grilled sandwiches.

Pea soup spiked with sour cream and Toasted Swiss Sandwiches join together for a hearty lunch. Spear sandwiches with radish roses on wooden picks for garnish.

Canned macaroni and cheese makes the creamy base for tasty Quick Tuna Salad.

Arrange filled tomato cups on lettuce leaves and garnish plate with pitted ripe olives.

CINNAMON TOAST COBBLER

    1 1-pound 14-ounce can (3½ cups) sliced peaches
    1 tablespoon cornstarch
    ¼ teaspoon salt
        • • •
    1 tablespoon lemon juice
    ¼ cup butter or margarine
        • • •
    3 slices slightly dry bread
    ¼ cup butter or margarine, melted
    ⅓ cup sugar
    ½ teaspoon ground cinnamon
    ¼ teaspoon ground nutmeg

Drain peaches, reserving 1 *cup* syrup. Combine cornstarch and salt; slowly blend in reserved syrup. Cook and stir till mixture comes to boiling. Reduce heat; cook and stir 2 minutes. Add lemon juice, ¼ cup butter, and peaches. Heat *just* to bubbling. Turn into 10x6x1½-inch baking dish.

Cut bread lengthwise into 1-inch strips; dip into ¼ cup melted butter, then into a mixture of sugar, cinnamon, and nutmeg. Arrange over hot peaches. Bake at 375° for 25 minutes or till toasty. Pass cream. Makes 6 servings.

QUICK TUNA SALAD

A salad with a quick new twist—

Combine one 1-pound can (2 cups) macaroni and cheese, one 6½- or 7-ounce can tuna, drained and flaked, one 8-ounce can peas, drained, ⅓ cup mayonnaise, 2 hard-cooked eggs, chopped, 1 tablespoon chopped green pepper, 1 teaspoon instant minced onion, ¼ teaspoon salt, and dash pepper; chill.

Cut 6 chilled medium tomatoes in sixths, to within ½ inch of bottom of the tomato. Spread the wedges apart.

Sprinkle inside of each tomato cup with salt, then fill with salad mixture. Serves 6.

 **MENU**

Quick Tuna Salad
Corn Muffins
Olives   Pickles
Cinnamon Toast Cobbler
Coffee   Tea

A combination of convenience foods will give you wonderful home-cooked flavor in old-fashioned Meat and Vegetable Soup. If desired, garnish servings with popped corn.

MEAT AND VEGETABLE SOUP

    1 envelope *dry* onion soup mix
    1 1-pound can meat balls with
      gravy
    1 1-pound can cream-style corn
    1 10¾-ounce can condensed tomato
      soup

Prepare the onion soup mix according to package directions. Add meat balls with gravy, corn, and tomato soup; stir till blended; heat through. Makes 6 to 8 servings.

PARMESAN MELBA TOAST

    French bread, sliced ¼ inch thick
    Softened butter or margarine
    Grated Parmesan cheese

Spread slices of bread with butter; sprinkle with cheese. Place on rack over a baking sheet. Bake in a slow oven (325°) about 20 minutes, or till bread is very crispy. Serve warm.

PINEAPPLE SALAD

In a screw top jar, combine 1 cup sweet French salad dressing, 1 teaspoon grated orange peel, and 2 tablespoons finely chopped chutney. Cover; shake; chill.

Drain one 1-pound 14-ounce can chilled pineapple slices. On individual salad plates, place 1 slice pineapple on crisp lettuce leaves. Top each slice with a mound of about ¼ cup drained cottage cheese.

Pour desired amount of dressing over the individual salads. Makes 6 to 8 servings.

 MENU

Meat and Vegetable Soup
Parmesan Melba Toast or *Crackers*
Pineapple Salad
Lime Sherbet   Sugar Cookies
Coffee   Milk

MENU

Chili-cheese Bake
Tossed Green Salad   *Italian Dressing*
Apricot Whip o*r* *Custard Sauced Berries*
Coffee   *Milk*

CHILI-CHEESE BAKE

  2 15-ounce cans chili with beans
30 to 32 rich round crackers
  1 4-ounce package (1 cup) shredded
      sharp Cheddar cheese
  2 teaspoons instant minced onion

Spoon a *third* of the canned chili over bottom of 10x6x1½-inch baking dish. Arrange *half* the crackers over chili; sprinkle with *half each* of the shredded cheese and onion. Repeat layers. Top with remaining chili.

Bake in a hot oven (400°) for 20 minutes, or until hot. Makes 6 servings.

APRICOT WHIP

  1 1-pound 14-ounce can
      peeled apricots
20 large marshmallows
  1 cup whipping cream, whipped

Drain apricots reserving ¼ cup syrup; remove pits. Blend apricots in blender or mash just till broken up. Combine apricots, marshmallows, and reserved syrup. Cook and stir till marshmallows are dissolved. Cool. Fold in whipped cream. Chill. Makes 6 servings.

CUSTARD SAUCED BERRIES

Prepare one 3¾- or 3⅝-ounce package *instant* vanilla pudding mix according to package directions, *but use 2½ cups milk.* Stir in ½ teaspoon vanilla. Chill about 30 minutes, or until mixture is the consistency of custard sauce. (If mixture gets too firm, beat with rotary beater till smooth.)

Serve over fresh strawberries, raspberries, or blueberries. Makes 2⅔ cups sauce.

DOUBLE CHEESE SANDWICHES

2 English muffins, halved and
    toasted
1 3-ounce package cream cheese
4 slices tomato
1 1-pound can asparagus spears,
    drained
    Dash garlic salt
    Dash pepper
    Dash instant minced onion
    Dash dried oregano, crushed
4 slices sharp process American
    cheese

Spread muffin halves evenly with cream cheese; place in 13x9x2-inch baking pan. Top each with a tomato slice and 3 asparagus spears. Combine seasonings; sprinkle over asparagus. Cover pan with foil; bake in moderate oven (375°) for 25 minutes. Uncover and top with cheese slices. Return to oven for 2 to 3 minutes or till cheese is melted. Garnish each with dairy sour cream and a pimiento-stuffed green olive half. Makes 4 servings.

BANANA-STRAWBERRY FREEZE

1 10-ounce package frozen
    strawberries, partially
    thawed
¼ cup lemon juice
1 fully-ripe banana, quartered
⅔ cup sugar
1 cup whipping cream, whipped

Break up frozen strawberries into blender container. Add lemon juice. Blend till smooth. Add banana and sugar; blend. Pour into mixing bowl; fold in whipped cream.

Freeze in refrigerator trays overnight, or till firm. Makes about 1 quart.

MENU

Double Cheese Sandwiches
Potato Chips   *Pickles*
Banana-strawberry Freeze
Coffee   *Milk*

RECIPES:
QUICK AND GOOD

When you're looking for ways to dress up convenience or packaged foods, this is the section to use. For everything from main dishes and salads to breads, soups, sandwiches, and desserts—you'll find plenty of ideas to make quick-fixing fare look tempting. Save those long-cooking classics that Mother taught you, for days when you have more time to spend in the kitchen. Instead, try a quick version of that classic using convenience products. Let automatic cooking appliances, such as blenders, help speed recipe preparation, too.

Throughout the book, you'll find Make Ahead Recipe symbols for foods that need chilling or freezing. Take advantage of these recipes and prepare them the day before or early in the day, when minutes are not so precious. Many other recipes, such as casseroles, can be prepared ahead of time and refrigerated, but remember to add a few extra minutes to the cooking time.

When unexpected company drops in, a well-stocked emergency shelf can save the day. Several recipes in this section use items that are stored on the shelf ready to be combined into delectable dishes for family or guests.

Serve Peach Pecan Mold with delicately spiced peach sauce right at the table for a perfect refreshing ending to a hearty meal. Both the mold and sauce can be made the day ahead to avoid last-minute rush. Garnish attractively with peach slices before serving.

MAIN DISHES IN MINUTES

TACO SALAD

1 pound ground beef
½ envelope (¼ cup) *dry* onion soup
    mix
¾ cup water
• • •
1 medium head lettuce, torn
    in bite-size pieces (about 4 cups)
1 large tomato, cut in wedges
1 small onion, thinly sliced and
    separated in rings
¼ cup chopped green pepper
½ cup sliced ripe olives
1 4-ounce package (1 cup) shredded
    sharp Cheddar cheese
1 6-ounce package corn chips

In skillet, brown ground beef. Sprinkle onion soup mix over meat; stir in the water. Simmer, uncovered, 10 minutes. In salad bowl, combine lettuce, tomato, onion, green pepper, olives, and cheese; toss well. Spoon on meat; top with corn chips. Makes 4 to 6 servings.

HERBED MEAT LOAF

1½ pounds ground beef
1 cup packaged herb-seasoned
    stuffing mix
1 8-ounce can tomato sauce
1 egg
1 teaspoon salt
¼ teaspoon pepper

Combine all ingredients; mix well. Shape in loaf in baking pan. Bake in a moderate oven (350°) about 1 hour. Makes 6 servings.

A main dish inspired by old Mexico

← Have a fiesta and serve Taco Salad with crusty hard rolls. Add a dash of bottled hot pepper sauce to meat mixture for extra zip.

BEEF IN MUSHROOM SAUCE

1 pound beef chuck, cut in 1-inch
    cubes
½ cup chopped onion
1 clove garlic, crushed
1 10¾-ounce can beef gravy
1 3-ounce can (⅔ cup) broiled
    sliced mushrooms (undrained)
¼ teaspoon dried basil, crushed
¼ cup claret

Trim excess fat from meat. Heat fat in skillet; when you have about 3 tablespoons melted fat, remove trimmings. Dredge meat in mixture of 2 tablespoons flour, ½ teaspoon monosodium glutamate, ¼ teaspoon salt, and dash pepper. Brown meat in hot fat; push meat to side of pan. Add onion and garlic; cook 3 minutes. Add gravy, mushrooms, and basil. Cover; simmer 45 to 50 minutes or till tender. Add claret. Serve over hot rice. Makes 4 servings.

HOW TO BROIL A STEAK

Broiling is best for tender steaks such as Sirloin, T-Bone, Rib, Tenderloin, Porterhouse, and for Ground Beef Patties. Steaks should be at least 1 inch thick for best flavor.

Slash fat edge of steak at 1-inch intervals to prevent meat from curling as it broils. Place steak on rack in broiler pan. Broil 1 to 1½-inch steaks so surface of meat is 3 inches from source of heat, thicker cuts 4 to 5 inches from source of heat.

Broil till desired degree of doneness, turning steak only once. Use tongs instead of fork to turn meat so juices don't escape.

Thickness of Steak	Rare	Medium	Well-done
		(total time in minutes)	
1 inch	8 to 10	12 to 14	18 to 20
1½ inch	14 to 16	18 to 20	25 to 30
2 inch	20 to 25	30 to 35	40 to 45
Ground beef Patties			
¾ inch	8	12	14

Minute steaks rolled around a bean and barbecue sauce mixture make Beef and Bean Roll-ups an unusual treat for your family.

BARBECUE PIZZA

This pizza is a breeze to make with canned barbecue sauce and refrigerated biscuits—

1 package refrigerated buttermilk
    biscuits (8 biscuits)
    Salad oil
1 1-pound can barbecue sauce and
    beef
    Dash dried oregano, crushed
    Dash garlic salt
½ cup shredded mozzarella cheese

Flatten biscuits into ovals and arrange around edge and in center of greased 12-inch pizza pan. Press together so entire bottom of pan is covered. Brush biscuits with oil. Spread barbecue sauce and beef over biscuits. Sprinkle with oregano and garlic salt. Top with cheese. Bake in hot oven (400°) 10 to 13 minutes, or till crust is browned. Makes 4 or 5 servings.

    Note: If desired, center pizza with a "rose" made by coiling folded canned red chilies for petals and twisting canned green chilies for "leaves." Center rose with ripe olive.

BEEF AND BEAN ROLL-UPS

6 minute or cube beef steaks
    Salt and pepper
6 tablespoons bottled barbecue sauce
6 tablespoons pickle relish
    • • •
1 1-pound can (2 cups) pork and
    beans in tomato sauce
3 tablespoons butter or margarine,
    melted

Pound steaks to flatten; sprinkle with salt and pepper. Spread *each* steak with 1 tablespoon barbecue sauce and top with 1 tablespoon pickle relish. Drain beans slightly; spoon onto steaks. Roll meat and fasten with wooden picks or skewers. Brush with melted butter and additional barbecue sauce. Broil for 10 minutes, turning once. Remove from broiler; season with salt and pepper. Serves 6.

EASY-DO MEAT LOAF

1 pound ground beef
2 tablespoons instant minced onion
¾ cup medium saltine cracker crumbs
    (about 18 crackers)
    Dash pepper
1 10½-ounce can condensed beef
    broth

Combine meat, onion, cracker crumbs, and pepper. Mix well. Add beef broth and mix till thoroughly blended. Turn into a greased 8½x 4½x2½-inch loaf dish. Bake in a moderate oven (350°) about 45 minutes. Serves 4.

SPANISH MEAT LOAF

1 pound ground beef
½ of 15-ounce can (1 cup) Spanish
    rice
1 egg
2 tablespoons instant minced onion
¼ teaspoon salt

Combine ground beef, Spanish rice, egg, onion, and salt. Shape into 4 or 5 individual loaves or put in 5 custard cups. Bake at 350° for 35 minutes. Makes 4 or 5 servings.

MEAL-IN-A-BOWL STEW ✓

1 pound ground beef
½ cup chopped onion
1 10½-ounce can condensed beef broth
1 1-pound can (2 cups) cream-style corn
3 large potatoes, pared and diced
1 teaspoon salt
Dash pepper

In skillet, brown ground beef and chopped onion. Add beef broth, cream-style corn, diced potatoes, salt, and pepper; mix well. Cover; cook over low heat for 20 to 25 minutes, stirring occasionally. Makes 4 or 5 servings.

CHILI AND DUMPLINGS

1 pound ground beef
¼ cup chopped green pepper
1 tablespoon instant minced onion
1 11-ounce can chili with beef soup
1 soup can water
1 8½-ounce package corn muffin mix
2 teaspoons dried parsley flakes
1 egg
⅓ cup milk

Brown ground beef in skillet. Drain off excess fat. Add green pepper, onion, chili soup, and water. Mix thoroughly and bring to boil. Combine muffin mix, parsley, egg, and milk; mix till well blended. Drop *half* the muffin mixture by tablespoons onto boiling chili to make 4 dumplings. (Bake remainder of mixture as muffins.) Cover tightly and simmer 15 minutes. Serve hot. Serves 4.

INSTANT PASTAFAZOOL

1 15-ounce can chili with beans
1 8-ounce can tomato sauce
7 ounces elbow macaroni, cooked
½ cup grated Parmesan cheese

Mix chili and tomato sauce; heat. Drain macaroni. Add to chili along with cheese. Toss to mix. Top with extra cheese. Serves 4 or 5.

GOURMET SAUCED STEAKS

4 to 6 steaks or ground meat patties
1 10½-ounce can mushroom gravy
1½ teaspoons soy sauce
¼ cup slivered almonds, toasted

Broil steaks or meat patties (see Index). Combine gravy and soy sauce; heat, stirring often. Stir in toasted almonds. Serve sauce over steaks or meat patties, and over potatoes or fluffy cooked rice. Makes 1¼ cups sauce.

ELEGANT VEAL

8 very thin slices veal (about 1 pound)
8 very thin slices prosciutto or cooked ham (about 6 ounces)
½ teaspoon dried sage, rubbed
2 tablespoons butter or margarine

• • •

Garlic salt
Thinly sliced lemon
3 tablespoons white wine
Snipped parsley

Pound veal slices paper thin. On each veal slice, place one slice of ham and a pinch of sage. Fold in half with ham inside; pat to seal. In hot butter in skillet, brown meat on both sides, about 2 minutes. Sprinkle with garlic salt and place a lemon slice on each. Add wine; simmer 5 minutes. Garnish with parsley. Makes 4 servings.

EASY CORNED BEEF HASH

1 7¼-ounce package dry hash brown potatoes
1 12-ounce can corned beef
½ envelope (¼ cup) *dry* onion soup mix
¼ cup butter or margarine

Cook hash brown potatoes according to package directions. Drain.

Add corned beef and dry onion soup mix; mix gently. Melt butter or margarine in a large skillet. Add potato mixture and fry till lightly browned. Makes about 6 servings.

SMOKED BEEF LUNCHEON

    1 10-ounce package frozen patty
       shells (6 shells)
             • • •
    1 envelope *dry* cream of leek soup mix
    1 6-ounce can evaporated milk
    3 drops bottled hot pepper sauce
    1 3½-ounce envelope smoked sliced
       beef, coarsely snipped
    2 tablespoons chopped canned
       pimiento

Bake shells according to package directions. Prepare soup according to package directions, *using 1¼ cups water and the 6-ounce can evaporated milk.* Stir in hot pepper sauce, beef, and pimiento; heat to boiling. Fill patty shells with hot beef mixture. Serves 6.

MEXICAN MIX-UPS

In large saucepan, combine one 15-ounce can tamales, cut in bite-size pieces, one 15-ounce can chili with beans, one 12-ounce can (1½ cups) whole kernel corn, and one 1-pound can (2 cups) tomatoes. Simmer, uncovered, for 25 to 30 minutes. Serve in bowls. Top each serving with about 2 tablespoons shredded sharp natural Cheddar cheese. Pass corn chips. Makes 4 to 6 servings.

No need to cook the macaroni before adding it to flavorful Easy Mexican Skillet. It cooks as the tomato sauce simmers slowly.

CHILI DON PEDRO

    2 10½-ounce cans chili without
       beans
    1 8-ounce package cream cheese
    1 12-ounce carton (1½ cups)
       cream-style cottage cheese
    ½ cup dairy sour cream
       Hot cornbread squares

Combine chili, cream cheese, and cottage cheese in saucepan; heat through, stirring to blend. Stir in sour cream and a dash salt; gently heat through, but do not boil. Serve over squares of hot cornbread. Serves 6 to 8.

ORANGE-GLAZED PORK CHOPS

    4 pork chops, ½ to ¾ inch thick
    ½ cup orange juice
    2 tablespoons brown sugar
    2 tablespoons orange marmalade
    1 tablespoon vinegar

In skillet, brown chops on both sides in small amount of hot fat; season with salt and pepper. Drain off excess fat. Combine remaining ingredients; pour over chops. Cover; simmer 45 to 50 minutes, or till chops are done. Remove chops to warm platter. Bring sauce to boiling; spoon over chops. Serves 4.

EASY MEXICAN SKILLET

    1 pound bulk pork sausage
    ¼ cup chopped onion
    ½ cup chopped green pepper
    1 cup uncooked elbow macaroni
    2 tablespoons sugar
    1 teaspoon salt
    1 teaspoon chili powder
    1 1-pound can (2 cups) tomatoes
    1 8-ounce can tomato sauce
    ½ cup dairy sour cream

Lightly brown meat; drain off excess fat. Add onion and green pepper; cook till tender. Stir in macaroni and next 5 ingredients. Cover and simmer 20 minutes. Stir in sour cream; heat through, but do not boil. Pass grated Parmesan cheese. Makes 5 servings.

SAUCY PORK CHOPS

6 pork chops, ½ to ¾ inch thick
Salt and pepper
1 medium onion, thinly sliced
1 10½-ounce can condensed cream
of chicken soup
¼ cup catsup
2 to 3 teaspoons Worcestershire
sauce

In skillet, brown chops on both sides in small amount of hot fat; season with salt and pepper. Top chops with onion slices. Combine remaining ingredients; pour over chops. Cover; simmer 45 to 60 minutes, or till chops are done. Remove chops to warm platter. Spoon sauce over. Makes 6 servings.

HAM WITH CHERRY SAUCE

1 fully cooked ham slice, ¾ to 1
inch thick (about 2 pounds)
1 1-pound 5-ounce can cherry pie
filling
¼ cup orange juice*
⅛ teaspoon ground ginger

Slash fat edge of ham slice. Place ham in 13x9x2-inch baking dish. Heat in moderate oven (350°) about 30 minutes. Serve with warm Cherry Sauce: In a saucepan, combine cherry pie filling with orange juice and ginger. Heat till mixture boils. Serves 6.

*Or, reduce the orange juice to 2 tablespoons and add 2 tablespoons lemon juice.

DILLED CREAMED EGGS

Blend one 10½-ounce can condensed cream of mushroom soup, one 10½-ounce can condensed cream of chicken soup, and 1 cup milk in saucepan. Combine 1 tablespoon cornstarch and 2 tablespoons cold water. Add to soup mixture. Bring to boiling and cook 3 minutes, stirring constantly.

Stir in one 3-ounce can sliced mushrooms, drained, 6 hard-cooked eggs, sliced, and ¼ teaspoon dillweed. Heat through. Just before serving, stir in ¼ cup sauterne. Heat, but do not boil. Serve over toasted English muffins. Garnish with parsley. Makes 6 servings.

QUICK TURKEY CURRY

Cook ¼ cup chopped onion in 1 tablespoon butter or margarine. Add one 10½-ounce can condensed cream of mushroom soup and ¼ cup milk; heat and stir till smooth. Stir in 1 cup dairy sour cream and ½ teaspoon curry powder. Add 1 cup cubed cooked turkey; heat, but do not boil. Garnish with snipped parsley. Serve over hot cooked rice. If desired, offer curry condiments of chutney, raisins, and toasted slivered almonds. Makes 4 servings.

EASY ITALIAN CHICKEN

1 2½- to 3 pound ready-to-cook
broiler-fryer chicken, cut up
½ cup butter or margarine, softened
½ envelope (1 tablespoon) garlic
salad dressing mix
1 cup corn flake crumbs
Paprika

Pat chicken dry with paper towels. Thoroughly combine butter and salad dressing mix. With spatula, spread butter mixture over chicken pieces. Roll in corn flake crumbs; sprinkle with paprika. Place pieces skin side up (not touching) in shallow pan. Bake in moderate oven (375°) about 1 hour or till tender—no need to turn. Makes 4 servings.

SPINACH-CHEESE FISH BAKE

1 11-ounce package frozen breaded
fish squares
1 10-ounce package frozen chopped
spinach
1 11-ounce can condensed Cheddar
cheese soup
2 tablespoons milk
Dash ground nutmeg
Lemon wedges

Arrange fish squares in a 10x6x1½-inch baking dish. Bake at 425° for 10 minutes. Meanwhile, cook frozen spinach according to package directions; drain. Combine drained spinach, cheese soup, milk, and nutmeg. Heat; spoon over fish in baking dish. Garnish with lemon wedges; return to oven for 5 minutes. Makes 4 to 6 servings.

46

HURRY TUNA SKILLET

1 7-ounce package macaroni and
   cheese dinner
3 tablespoons butter or margarine
1 8-ounce can tomatoes
1 6-ounce can evaporated milk
1 6½- or 7-ounce can tuna, drained
2 tablespoons instant minced onion
2 teaspoons parsley flakes

Cook macaroni from packaged dinner according to directions; drain. In skillet, toss macaroni with cheese (included in package) and butter. Add tomatoes, evaporated milk, tuna, onion, and parsley flakes. Season with salt and pepper to taste. Simmer, uncovered, about 5 minutes, stirring occasionally. Serves 5.

HERB-CRUMB TOPPED FISH

2 12-ounce packages frozen
   halibut steaks, thawed
¼ cup butter or margarine, melted
   Salt
   Pepper
       • • •
¼ cup dry bread crumbs
⅛ teaspoon dried thyme, crushed
   Dash garlic salt

Place fish on rack of broiler pan and brush with some of the melted butter or margarine. Season with salt and pepper. Broil 5 inches from heat for 5 minutes. Turn fish, brush with melted butter or margarine, and season with salt and pepper.

Broil 3 minutes. Add crumbs and seasonings to remaining butter or margarine. Sprinkle on fish. Return to broiler to brown crumbs, about 3 to 5 minutes. Makes 4 to 6 servings.

ZIPPY FISH FILLETS

Combine 2 tablespoons Worcestershire sauce and 1 tablespoon lemon juice. Cut 1 pound fish fillets in serving size pieces. Dip pieces in the lemon juice mixture; season with salt and pepper; dip in ½ cup dry bread crumbs. Bake in greased, shallow pan in an extremely hot oven (500°) about 15 minutes. Serve with lemon wedges or tartare sauce. Serves 4.

SHRIMP NEWBURG

8 frozen patty shells
2 10-ounce cans frozen cream of
   shrimp soup
1 cup milk
2 cups cooked shrimp
1 1-pound can peas, drained
¼ cup sherry
1 4-ounce package shredded sharp
   Cheddar cheese (1 cup)

Bake patty shells according to package directions. Combine soup and milk; heat. Add shrimp and peas and continue to heat, stirring, till just simmering. Cook slowly, about 5 minutes. Stir in the sherry and *half* the cheese. (Sprinkle remaining cheese in baked patty shells.) To serve, spoon sauce into patty shells. Makes 8 servings.

TUNA STROGANOFF

Soften 1 tablespoon instant minced onion in 2 tablespoons water. In medium saucepan, blend one 10½-ounce can condensed cream of mushroom soup, the softened onion, and dash pepper. Add one 6½- or 7-ounce can tuna, drained, one 3-ounce can sliced mushrooms, drained (½ cup), and 1 tablespoon chopped canned pimiento. Bring to boiling. Stir in ½ cup dairy sour cream. Heat, but do not boil. Serve over hot cooked noodles. Serves 4.

CURRIED TUNA AND PEAS

Blend ½ cup milk into one 10½-ounce can condensed cream of mushroom soup. Add ½ to 1 teaspoon curry powder and heat to boiling. Carefully stir in one 6½- or 7-ounce can tuna, drained, and 1 cup frozen peas. Cover and simmer 5 minutes. Serve over hot cooked rice. Makes 4 servings.

An elegant luncheon or supper dish

Prepare an easy version of classic Shrimp →
Newburg. Serve it over baked patty shells with cheese sprinkled inside for a surprise.

SAUCY FRANKS

As shown on the cover—

- 1 pound frankfurters (8 to 10)
- 2 tablespoons butter or margarine
- 1 10¾-ounce can condensed tomato soup
- ¼ cup brown sugar
- ¼ cup water
- 3 tablespoons vinegar
- 1 tablespoon Worcestershire sauce
- ½ lemon, thinly sliced
- ½ onion, thinly sliced
- ¼ cup chopped green pepper

Score franks in corkscrew fashion. In skillet, brown franks lightly in butter. Add remaining ingredients except green pepper. Simmer covered about 10 minutes. Add green pepper and cook covered 5 minutes longer. Serve over hot cooked noodles or over buns. Serves 4 or 5.

SQUAW CORN

Dice one 12-ounce can luncheon meat. In skillet, brown meat and 2 tablespoons chopped onion. Add one 1-pound can golden cream-style corn; heat till bubbly. Stir in 3 beaten eggs. Cook over low heat, stirring occasionally, just till eggs are set. Serve immediately sprinkled with snipped chives, if desired. Makes 6 servings.

SKILLET BARBECUE

- ½ cup chopped onion
- 2 tablespoons butter or margarine
- 1 cup catsup
- ⅓ cup water
- ¼ cup brown sugar
- 3 tablespoons vinegar
- 1 tablespoon prepared mustard
- 1 tablespoon Worcestershire sauce
- 1 12-ounce can luncheon meat, cut in julienne strips

Cook onion in butter till tender, but not brown. Stir in catsup and next 6 ingredients. Simmer uncovered 15 minutes. Serve over hot cooked rice or on toasted hamburger buns. Makes 6 servings.

FRANK AND CABBAGE SUPPER

- 1 medium head cabbage, cut in wedges
- 1 pound frankfurters (8 to 10)
- 1 envelope cheese sauce mix
- 2 tablespoons prepared mustard
  Dash bottled hot pepper sauce

Cook cabbage, covered, in small amount of boiling water for 10 minutes; add franks and cook till cabbage is tender, 3 to 4 minutes more. Meanwhile, prepare cheese sauce according to package directions; stir in mustard and hot pepper sauce. Serve sauce over cabbage wedges. Makes 4 or 5 servings.

YAM AND SAUSAGE SKILLET

- 1 8-ounce package brown and serve sausage links
- 1 3-ounce package orange-flavored gelatin
- ¼ cup brown sugar
- 2 tablespoons butter or margarine
- 1 teaspoon instant minced onion
- 2 teaspoons dry mustard
- 1 teaspoon grated lemon peel
- 3 tablespoons lemon juice
- ¼ teaspoon salt
  Dash pepper
- 1 1-pound 4-ounce can yams, drained
- 1 1-pound 4½-ounce can pineapple chunks, drained
  Snipped parsley

In large skillet, brown sausage as directed on package. Remove sausage. In same skillet, combine gelatin with ½ cup water and next 8 ingredients. Heat, stirring constantly, till mixture is boiling. Add yams and pineapple. Reduce heat and simmer gently 15 minutes, basting often with sauce. Add sausage; continue to cook, basting frequently, for 5 minutes. Sprinkle with parsley. Serves 4 or 5.

Be creative with convenience foods

Orange-flavored gelatin glazes and glamorizes this quick supper of Yam and Sausage Skillet. And what it adds to the flavor! →

HAMBURGER STROGANOFF

    1 pound ground beef
    2 tablespoons all-purpose flour
    1 tablespoon instant minced onion
    1 beef bouillon cube
    ½ teaspoon garlic salt
    ½ teaspoon paprika
    1 3-ounce can sliced mushrooms
    1 envelope sour cream sauce mix
    1 6-ounce can evaporated milk
    2 tablespoons sherry

Brown meat in 2 tablespoons butter. Stir in flour and next 4 ingredients. Add 1 cup water and mushrooms with liquid. Cover; simmer 10 minutes. Combine sauce mix with milk; stir into meat mixture. Add wine; heat through. Serve over hot buttered noodles. Serves 4 to 6.

CHUCK WAGON MACARONI

    1 7-ounce package macaroni
    ½ cup butter or margarine
    ¼ cup chili sauce
    1 teaspoon Worcestershire sauce
        • • •
    ½ pound sharp process American
      cheese, shredded (2 cups)
      Paprika

In large saucepan, cook macaroni according to package directions; drain well. Return cooked macaroni to saucepan; add butter or margarine, chili sauce, and Worcestershire sauce; heat till butter is melted. Add shredded cheese; stir till melted and well mixed. Sprinkle with paprika, if desired. Serve immediately. Makes 4 to 6 servings.

Hamburger Stroganoff is an easier and less expensive version of a classic recipe. Trim top with sliced green onions. The perfect accompaniment is a tossed green salad.

CONVENIENT CASSEROLES

SMOKED BEEF AND MACARONI

1 3½-ounce package sliced smoked
  beef, snipped (1 cup)
1 15-ounce can (2 cups) macaroni
  and cheese
1 3-ounce can chopped mushrooms,
  drained (½ cup)
2 ounces sharp natural Cheddar
  cheese, shredded (½ cup)
¼ cup chopped green pepper
1 hard-cooked egg, chopped
1 tablespoon instant minced onion
½ teaspoon Worcestershire sauce
½ cup soft bread crumbs
2 tablespoons butter or margarine,
  melted

Combine all ingredients except crumbs and
butter or margarine; turn into 1-quart casserole. Combine crumbs and butter; sprinkle
over top. Bake, uncovered, in moderate oven
(350°) for 35 to 40 minutes. Garnish with
green pepper rings or hard-cooked egg slices,
if desired. Makes 4 servings.

JIFFY CHILI-HOMINY BAKE

1 pound ground beef
½ cup chopped onion
1 15-ounce can (2 cups) chili
  with beans
1 tablespoon chili powder
1 10½-ounce can condensed cream
  of chicken soup
1 1-pound 4-ounce can (2½ cups)
  yellow hominy, drained
2 tablespoons sliced ripe olives
2 ounces process American
  cheese, shredded (½ cup)

Cook beef and onion till meat is browned. Stir
in remaining ingredients, except cheese. Turn
into 2-quart casserole. Cover; bake at 350° for
25 minutes. Sprinkle cheese over top; bake uncovered 5 minutes longer. Serves 6.

MEXICAN SUPPER CASSEROLE

¼ cup chopped onion
¼ cup chopped green pepper
1 tablespoon butter or margarine
2 15-ounce cans (4 cups) chili
  with beans
1 12-ounce can (1½ cups) whole
  kernel corn, drained
1 4½-ounce can (¾ cup) chopped
  ripe olives
1 4-ounce package (1 cup) shredded
  sharp Cheddar cheese
1 package corn muffin mix

In large skillet, cook onion and pepper in butter till tender. Stir in chili, corn, and olives;
bring to boiling. Add cheese; stir to melt.
Pour into 11x7x1½-inch baking pan.

Prepare muffin mix according to package
directions. Spoon dough in diagonal bands
across top of casserole; (bake any remaining
dough in muffin pans and freeze for later use).
Bake at 400° for 15 to 20 minutes. Serves 8.

BOLOGNA-NOODLE BAKE

1 10¾-ounce can condensed
  tomato soup
½ cup milk
⅓ cup chopped ripe olives
1 tablespoon vinegar
4 ounces (2 cups) medium noodles,
  cooked and drained
1½ to 2 teaspoons chili powder
7 or 8 slices bologna, quartered
4 ounces sharp process
  American cheese, shredded (1 cup)
1 cup corn chips, slightly crushed

Combine soup and milk; add next 4 ingredients. Place *half* the mixture in 10x6x1½-inch
baking dish. Top with *half* the meat and *half*
the cheese. Repeat layers. Bake at 350° for 25
minutes. Top with corn chips; bake 15 minutes longer. Makes 4 or 5 servings.

HAMBURGER AND MACARONI

Combine in a 2½-quart casserole 1 pound ground beef, one 10½-ounce can condensed chicken-rice soup, one 10½-ounce can condensed beef broth, one 1-pound 1-ounce can cream-style corn, ¼ cup chopped green pepper, 2 tablespoons instant minced onion, one 7-ounce package elbow macaroni, and ½ teaspoon salt; mix well. Cover and bake at 375° for 1 hour. Uncover; top with toasted croutons. Bake 10 minutes longer. Serves 6.

BEEF AND CHEESE BAKE

- 1½ pounds ground beef
- ½ cup chopped onion
- 1 8-ounce package cream cheese, softened
- ¼ cup milk
- 1 10½-ounce can condensed cream of mushroom soup
- ⅓ cup ripe olives, sliced
- ¼ cup catsup
- 1 teaspoon salt
- 1 package refrigerated biscuits (10 biscuits)

Brown ground beef and onion in skillet. Meanwhile, blend cream cheese and milk together. Stir in soup, olives, catsup, and salt. Combine with meat and onion in 2-quart casserole. Bake at 375° for 30 minutes. Arrange biscuits on top and bake 15 minutes longer, or till biscuits are browned. Serves 6.

ENCHILADA CASSEROLE

Reserve 1 cup of a 6-ounce package corn chips for topper. Combine remaining chips with 6 ounces sharp process American cheese, shredded (1½ cups), one 15-ounce can chili with beans, one 15-ounce can enchilada sauce, one 8-ounce can tomato sauce, and 1 tablespoon instant minced onion. Pour into 11x7x 1½-inch baking pan.

Bake uncovered at 375° for 30 minutes or till hot. Spread top of mixture with 1 cup dairy sour cream. Sprinkle with ½ cup additional shredded sharp process American cheese. Circle reserved corn chips around edge. Bake 5 minutes longer. Makes 6 servings.

MEXICAN CASSEROLE

- 1 10½-ounce can condensed cream of chicken soup
- ½ 8-ounce jar (½ cup) pasteurized process cheese spread
- ½ cup milk
- 2 5-ounce cans boned chicken, diced
- ¼ cup canned green chilies, chopped
- 1 tablespoon instant minced onion
- 1 6-ounce package (about 6 cups) corn chips

Combine soup, cheese, and milk. Beat with rotary beater till smooth. Stir in chicken, chilies, and onion. In a 10x6x1½-inch baking dish, layer *half* the corn chips and *half* the cheese mixture. Repeat layers ending with cheese mixture. Bake uncovered at 350° about 30 minutes. Makes 4 or 5 servings.

TURKEY RICE BAKE

- 1 cup long-grain rice
- 3 tablespoons butter or margarine, melted
- 1 10½-ounce can condensed onion soup
- 1⅓ cups water
- ½ cup chopped green pepper
- ½ cup diced celery
- 2 5-ounce cans boned turkey
- 1 3-ounce can sliced mushrooms, drained (½ cup)
- 2 slices process American cheese, halved diagonally
- Sliced ripe olives

Add rice to the melted butter or margarine in large skillet, and brown over medium heat, stirring occasionally. Blend in onion soup and water; cover and cook 10 minutes. Add green pepper and celery; cook, covered, 10 to 15 minutes longer, or till rice is tender, stirring occasionally. Add the turkey and the sliced mushrooms; mix well. Transfer to a greased 1½-quart casserole.

Bake in moderate oven (350°) 15 to 20 minutes, or till heated through. Remove casserole from oven; top with the halved cheese slices, forming a pinwheel design, and return to oven for a few minutes, till cheese begins to melt. Garnish with sliced ripe olives. Serves 6.

DUBLIN DILLY HOT DISH

1 12-ounce can corned beef, cubed
1 1-pound can (2 cups) peas and onions, drained
1 envelope chicken gravy mix
¼ teaspoon dried dillweed
• • •
Packaged instant mashed potatoes (enough for 4 servings)
2 ounces sharp process American cheese, shredded (½ cup)

Combine corned beef with peas and onions in a 1½-quart casserole. Prepare gravy mix according to package directions; add dillweed. Stir into meat mixture.

Prepare potatoes according to package directions. Top vegetable-beef mixture with a ring of mashed potatoes. Bake in a moderate oven (375°) for 20 minutes. Sprinkle cheese on top; bake 5 minutes longer or till cheese is melted. Makes 4 to 6 servings.

NEWBURG NOODLES

1 10-ounce can frozen cream of shrimp soup
1 6-ounce can (⅔ cup) evaporated milk
• • •
⅓ cup mayonnaise or salad dressing
2 ounces sharp natural Cheddar cheese, shredded (½ cup)
¼ teaspoon salt
• • •
¼ cup dry white wine
4 ounces noodles, cooked and drained
1 4½-ounce can shrimp, drained
½ cup crushed potato chips

Heat soup and milk in medium saucepan till boiling, stirring occasionally. Remove from heat. Add mayonnaise, cheese, and salt; stir till cheese melts. Blend in wine.

Add to cooked noodles along with drained shrimp; mix well. Bake, covered, in a 1½-quart casserole in moderate oven (350°) for 25 minutes. Uncover; top with crushed potato chips and return to oven for 5 minutes longer. Makes 4 to 6 servings.

TUNA-RICE BAKE

1 6½- or 7-ounce can tuna
1 10½-ounce can condensed cream of celery soup
¾ cup packaged precooked rice
2 slightly beaten egg yolks
¼ cup milk
1 tablespoon lemon juice
2 tablespoons chopped canned pimiento
2 teaspoons instant minced onion
2 stiffly beaten egg whites
½ cup milk
1 tablespoon snipped parsley

Drain tuna; break in chunks. Combine with *half* the soup, rice, egg yolks, ¼ cup milk, lemon juice, pimiento, and onion. Fold in egg whites. Turn into a greased 10x6x1½-inch baking dish. Bake in a moderate oven (350°) for 20 to 25 minutes, or till set.

Serve with Parsley Sauce: Heat remaining soup with ½ cup milk and the snipped parsley. Makes 6 servings.

TUNA ORIENTAL

Combine one 6½- or 7-ounce can tuna, drained and flaked, two 15-ounce cans macaroni and cheese, one 11-ounce can mandarin oranges, drained, one 3-ounce can chopped mushrooms, drained, 2 tablespoons instant minced onion, and 1 teaspoon parsley flakes.

Turn into a 10x6x1½-inch baking dish. Top with one 3-ounce can chow mein noodles. Bake at 350° about 35 minutes. Serves 6.

FRANK HASH-BROWN BAKE

In a 2-quart casserole, gradually stir ½ cup milk into one 10½-ounce can condensed cream of celery soup. Add ½ teaspoon salt, dash pepper, 1 teaspoon prepared mustard, one 1-pound can cut green beans, drained, ½ cup canned French fried onions, one 12-ounce package frozen hash brown potatoes, thawed, and ½ pound frankfurters, sliced (4 or 5).

Cover. Bake in moderate oven (350°) 45 to 50 minutes or till potatoes are done. Uncover and top with ½ cup canned French fried onions. Return to oven for 5 minutes. Serves 4.

Tasty Chevron Rice Bake features canned luncheon meat in a topnotch way! Clove-studded peaches add flair to the curry-rice mixture—perfect for serving to a group.

CHEVRON RICE BAKE

    2 12-ounce cans luncheon meat
    4 cups cooked rice
    1 10-ounce package frozen peas,
       thawed
    2 slightly beaten eggs
    1 10½-ounce can condensed cream
       of chicken soup
    ½ cup milk
    ¼ cup snipped parsley
    ¼ cup chopped onion
    1 teaspoon curry powder
    1 1-pound 14-ounce can peach
       halves, drained

Slice contents of *one* can luncheon meat; reserve for top. Cut contents of other can in ½-inch cubes. Combine with remaining ingredients except peaches; add dash pepper. Spread in 13x9x2-inch baking dish. Stud peach halves with whole cloves; arrange with sliced meat atop rice-meat mixture. Bake at 350° for 40 to 45 minutes or till hot. Serves 8.

MEAT AND MACARONI SUPPER

    ½ cup chopped onion
    2 tablespoons butter, melted
    1 10½-ounce can condensed cream
       of celery soup
    1 8-ounce can tomatoes, cut up
    ¼ teaspoon dried thyme, crushed
    ½ 7-ounce package (1 cup) elbow
       macaroni, cooked and drained
    1 12-ounce can luncheon meat, cut
       in 1x½-inch strips
    ¼ cup chopped green pepper
    ¼ cup shredded process American
       cheese

In medium skillet, cook onion in butter till tender, but not brown. Stir in the soup, tomatoes, thyme, and dash pepper. Add the cooked macaroni, luncheon meat, and green pepper. Spoon into 1½-quart casserole. Top with shredded cheese. Bake, uncovered, in moderate oven (350°) for 35 to 40 minutes or till heated through. Makes 4 to 6 servings.

GINGER BEANS WITH LUNCHEON MEAT

    2 1-pound cans pork and beans in
       tomato sauce
    ½ cup finely crushed gingersnaps
    ¼ cup catsup
    2 tablespoons light molasses
    ½ teaspoon salt
    1 12-ounce can luncheon meat

Combine beans, gingersnap crumbs, catsup, molasses, and salt; turn into 1-quart casserole. Cut luncheon meat in six slices; place on top of beans. Bake, covered, in moderate oven (350°) for 30 minutes. Makes 4 to 6 servings.

ONE-DISH MEAL

Combine one 1-pound can whole green beans, drained, ¼ teaspoon dried basil, crushed, and ¼ teaspoon salt. Pile in center of 10-inch pie plate. Combine one 15-ounce can macaroni and cheese, 1 teaspoon prepared mustard, and 1 teaspoon Worcestershire sauce; surround beans with mixture. Place one 4-ounce can Vienna sausages, cut in halves lengthwise, spoke fashion on macaroni. Brush beans and sausages with 1 tablespoon melted butter. Sprinkle with 2 tablespoons grated Parmesan cheese. Bake at 350° for 15 to 20 minutes or till hot. Serves 3 or 4.

MEXICALI CASSEROLE

    1 1-pound 4-ounce can (2½ cups)
       yellow hominy, drained
    1 15-ounce can tamales, cut in
       thirds
    1 4-ounce can Vienna sausages, cut
       in thirds
    1 10½-ounce can condensed cream
       of chicken soup
    1 ounce sharp natural Cheddar cheese,
       shredded (¼ cup)

Combine hominy, tamales, the Vienna sausages, and soup. Gently mix; turn into 1½-quart casserole. Bake, uncovered, at 350° for 35 to 40 minutes. Sprinkle cheese over top; return to oven for a few minutes to melt the cheese. Makes 6 servings.

FRANK-VEGETABLE MEDLEY

    ½ pound frankfurters (4 or 5),
       cut in 1-inch pieces
    ½ cup long-grain rice
    1 8-ounce can tomato sauce
    1 cup water
    1 10-ounce package frozen mixed
       vegetables, slightly thawed
    ¼ cup chopped onion
    1 teaspoon salt
       Dash bottled hot pepper sauce

Combine frankfurters with remaining ingredients in 2-quart casserole, breaking up frozen vegetables with fork. Bake, covered, at 375° for 1 hour or till heated through. Stir once or twice during baking time. Serves 6.

SCALLOPED DEVILED HAM

    6 slices slightly dry bread
    1 4½-ounce can deviled ham
    1 4-ounce package shredded sharp
       natural Cheddar cheese (1 cup)
    1½ teaspoons instant minced onion
    2 cups milk
    3 slightly beaten eggs
    ¼ teaspoon salt
       Dash pepper

Trim crusts from bread; spread slices with deviled ham. Arrange in greased 10x6x1½-inch baking dish; sprinkle with cheese and onion. Combine remaining ingredients; pour over top. Bake at 350° for 30 minutes or till knife inserted comes out clean. Let stand 10 minutes. Makes 4 to 6 servings.

SWEET POTATO FANTASIA

Prepare two 3¼-ounce packages *or* two 3½-ounce cans instant sweet potatoes according to package directions; cool.

Stir in 1 slightly beaten egg, 2 tablespoons brown sugar, and ¼ teaspoon salt. Fold in ½ cup seedless green grapes and ¼ cup broken pecans. Pile into 1-quart casserole. Bake, uncovered, in a moderate oven (350°) for 25 minutes. Top with ½ pound sliced Canadian-style bacon. Return to oven; bake 15 minutes longer. Makes 4 to 6 servings.

Cleanup is simple with Easy Perfection Salad, made right in the mold. Ice cubes speed the chilling of the gelatin so that it's just right for adding vegetables.

A quick and easy way to prepare the sauerkraut is to use kitchen shears and snip the kraut while it's still in the can.

MAKE AHEAD RECIPE

EASY PERFECTION SALAD

Place the contents of two 3-ounce packages lemon-flavored gelatin in an 8½x4½x2½-inch loaf dish. Add 2 cups boiling water and stir to dissolve gelatin. Add 1 tablespoon vinegar and 12 to 15 ice cubes; stir constantly till gelatin begins to thicken (about 3 minutes). Remove any unmelted ice.

Snip into the partially set gelatin the tops of 6 or 7 small green onions and 1 pimiento. Cut through the contents of one 1-pound can (2 cups) sauerkraut. Add sauerkraut to gelatin; stir gently to distribute vegetables. Chill till set, about 4 hours or overnight. Unmold onto crisp greens on a serving plate. Garnish.

Serve with Horseradish Mayonnaise: Stir 1 teaspoon prepared horseradish into 1 cup mayonnaise or salad dressing. Serves 8 to 10.

TASTY SALADS AND VEGETABLES

STRAWBERRY YOGURT SALAD

You'd never guess what you were eating in this delectable salad mold—

1 8¾-ounce can crushed pineapple
1 envelope (1 tablespoon) unflavored gelatin
1 8-ounce carton (1 cup) strawberry-flavored yogurt
Dash salt
1 10-ounce package frozen straw-berries, thawed

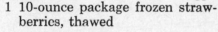

Drain pineapple, reserving syrup. Soften gelatin in the pineapple syrup. Stir over low heat till gelatin is dissolved. Stir into strawberry-flavored yogurt with dash salt. Add thawed strawberries including syrup and drained pineapple. Mix well. Pour into 1-quart mold; chill till set. Unmold onto lettuce. Garnish with more strawberries. Makes 4 to 6 servings.

CREAMY ASPIC

1 envelope (1 tablespoon) unflavored gelatin
1 12-ounce can vegetable-juice cocktail
• • •
1 3-ounce package cream cheese, softened
1 teaspoon lemon juice
½ teaspoon Worcestershire sauce
¼ teaspoon onion juice

In a saucepan, soften gelatin in *half* of the vegetable-juice cocktail. Stir over low heat till gelatin is dissolved. Remove from heat and beat in cream cheese with rotary beater. Stir in remaining cocktail, lemon juice, Worcestershire sauce, and onion juice.

Pour into 3-cup mold. Chill till firm. Unmold on crisp greens. Makes 4 servings.

APRICOT FRUIT SALAD

An easy version of 24-hour salad—

1 1-pound 6-ounce can apricot pie filling
1 11-ounce can mandarin oranges, drained
1 1-pound 14-ounce can pineapple chunks, drained
1 8½-ounce can grapefruit sections, drained
1 cup miniature marshmallows
2 bananas, sliced

Have all fruits chilled (except bananas). Combine all ingredients in large bowl. Garnish with lettuce and maraschino cherries or make individual servings. Serves 10 to 12.

DELLA ROBBIA SALAD

A colorful arrangement of fruit—

Drain one 1-pound 13-ounce can chilled peach halves, and two 1-pound cans chilled pear halves. Arrange bed of crisp salad greens on large round plate. Around outer rim, place pear and peach halves in pairs so as to resemble whole fruit. (A little fluffy cream cheese spread on cut sides of peach and pear halves will make them hold together well and will add flavor.)

Drain one 1-pound 4½-ounce can chilled pineapple slices. Cut in halves. Place two half slices between each pear and peach.

Drain one 1-pound 1-ounce can chilled peeled whole apricots and one 1-pound jar chilled spiced crab apples. Arrange apricots and crab apples alternately in inner circle. Place chilled seedless green grapes in center and garnish with sprig of mint or holly.

Serve with salad dressing of dairy sour cream thinned slightly with some of the syrup from the canned fruit. Serves 10 to 12.

Pureeing canned apricots in an electric blender gets tantalizing Orange Apricot Ring off to a quick and easy beginning.

CURRY AVOCADO SALAD

    1 beef bouillon cube
    1 cup mayonnaise
    ½ teaspoon curry powder
    2 large avocados, peeled and sliced
      Bibb lettuce

Dissolve bouillon cube in 3 tablespoons boiling water. Add mayonnaise and curry powder. Chill. Serve over avocado slices on lettuce. (Dip avocado slices in lemon or pineapple juice to keep color fresh.) Makes 8 salads.

PEANUT-MALLOW DRESSING

    ½ pint jar marshmallow creme
    ¼ cup orange juice
    ½ cup peanut butter
    ¼ cup mayonnaise or salad dressing
    1 tablespoon lemon juice

Combine marshmallow creme and orange juice; whip till very fluffy with electric beater. Blend peanut butter, mayonnaise, and lemon juice; fold into marshmallow mixture. Serve over fresh or canned fruit. Makes 2 cups.

ORANGE APRICOT RING

    1 1-pound can apricot halves
    2 3-ounce packages orange-flavored gelatin
    1 6-ounce can frozen orange juice concentrate
    1 cup cold water

Drain apricots, reserving syrup. Puree apricots in electric blender. Add enough water to reserved syrup to make 1½ cups. Combine reserved syrup, gelatin, and dash salt; heat to boiling, stirring to dissolve gelatin. Remove from heat. Add concentrate and stir till melted. Stir in apricot puree and water. Pour into 5-cup ring mold and chill till firm.

Unmold on lettuce. If desired, fill center with lettuce and orange sections. Arrange orange sections and frosted grapes around mold. Makes 8 to 10 servings.

CURRIED APPLE RELISH

Melt 2 tablespoons butter or margarine in medium skillet. Stir in 1 teaspoon sugar and ½ teaspoon curry powder.

Add one 1-pound 4-ounce can pie-sliced apples, drained; toss to coat with curry mixture. Cook, stirring occasionally, over low heat till apples are heated through, about 5 minutes. Serve as relish with meat. Serves 6 to 8.

BAKED CHUTNEY PEACHES

Place 6 canned peach halves cut side up on rack. Brush with 1 tablespoon melted butter or margarine. Spoon 1 tablespoon chutney into center of each peach half. Place in baking dish and bake at 350° for 10 to 15 minutes or till heated. Serve hot. Serves 6.

SELF-PICKLING ONIONS

Slice 1 or 2 medium onions in ¼-inch slices. Separate in rings and drop into a jar of pickle juice—be sure there is enough juice to cover onions. Either dill-pickle or sweet-pickle juice works fine. Refrigerate onions 2 or 3 days to pickle. Delicious with hamburgers or in a tossed green salad.

GREEN BEAN SALAD

1 9-ounce package frozen French-
   style green beans, thawed
1 medium onion, thinly sliced and
   separated in rings
1 3-ounce can sliced mushrooms,
   drained (½ cup)
⅓ cup Italian salad dressing
¼ teaspoon salt
   Dash freshly ground pepper
2 medium tomatoes, cut in wedges

Pour boiling water over beans; let stand about 5 minutes; drain thoroughly. Place in salad bowl with onion rings and mushrooms. Combine salad dressing, salt, and pepper. Add to salad and toss. Marinate in refrigerator at least 2 hours, tossing occasionally. Just before serving, arrange the tomato wedges on salad. Makes 4 to 6 servings.

MARINATED SALAD

Cook one 10-ounce package frozen cauliflower according to package directions; drain well. Cool and cut into buds. Drain well one 1-pound can (2 cups) *each* of julienne carrots, cut green beans, peas, and artichoke hearts, halved. Arrange with cauliflower and 1 cup chopped celery in large salad bowl.

Add 1 tablespoon instant minced onion to ½ cup French salad dressing; drizzle over vegetables. Marinate 1 hour. Serves 10 to 12.

Dress with Chili-dill Dressing: Blend ¾ cup mayonnaise or salad dressing with ¼ cup chili sauce, 2 teaspoons dried dillweed, 1 teaspoon salt, dash pepper, and 1 tablespoon lemon juice. Chill before serving.

HOT POTATO SALAD FIX-UP

2 1-pound cans German-style
   potato salad
8 slices bacon, cooked and
   coarsely crumbled
4 ounces sharp process American
   cheese, diced (1 cup)

Combine all ingredients in a 1½-quart casserole. Bake, uncovered, in a slow oven (300°) for 25 to 30 minutes. Serve hot. Serves 6.

FRANK AND POTATO SALAD

½ pound frankfurters (4 or 5),
   cut in ½-inch pieces
1 tablespoon butter or margarine
   • • •
½ envelope (¼ cup) *dry* onion
   soup mix
1 tablespoon all-purpose flour
1 tablespoon sugar
   Dash pepper
½ cup water
2 tablespoons vinegar
   • • •
2 1-pound cans (4 cups) sliced
   white potatoes, drained
½ cup dairy sour cream

Brown frankfurters in butter or margarine; remove from heat. Stir in onion soup mix, flour, sugar, and pepper. Add water and vinegar. Return to heat; cook and stir till boiling. Reduce heat and simmer gently, covered, for 10 minutes. Add the drained, sliced potatoes and dairy sour cream; heat just to boiling. Serve hot. Makes 6 servings.

The potatoes for Frank and Potato Salad come ready-cooked and sliced, right from the can. Onion soup mix adds the flavoring.

POTATOES ALASKA

Packaged instant mashed potatoes
(enough for 4 servings)
2 tablespoons butter or margarine
2 egg yolks
2 tablespoons chopped green
onion tops
½ teaspoon salt
Dash pepper

• • •

2 egg whites
2 tablespoons mayonnaise or
salad dressing
½ teaspoon lemon juice

Prepare instant mashed potatoes according to package directions, *omitting the milk called for.* Add butter or margarine, egg yolks, green onion tops, salt, and pepper to mashed potatoes; mix well.

Spoon 6 mounds onto foil-covered baking sheet. Beat egg whites till stiff peaks form; fold in mayonnaise and lemon juice. Top each potato mound with egg white mixture. Bake in moderate oven (350°) for 10 to 12 minutes or till egg whites are golden. Makes 6 servings.

Potatoes Alaska have a tasty "snow cap" of egg white and mayonnaise over the fluffy potatoes made from a packaged product.

CREAMY HASH BROWN BAKE

1 10½-ounce can condensed cream of
celery soup
⅓ cup milk
1 3-ounce package cream cheese

• • •

4 cups loose-pack frozen hash
brown potatoes
1 8-ounce can (1 cup) small whole
onions, drained and cut in pieces

• • •

2 ounces sharp process American
cheese, shredded (½ cup)

In saucepan, combine soup, milk, and cream cheese; cook and stir over medium heat till smooth. Combine potatoes and onions; stir in soup mixture. Pour into 10x6x1½-inch baking dish; cover with foil. Bake at 350° for 1¼ hours, or till potatoes are tender. Remove foil; top with shredded cheese. Return to oven to melt cheese. Makes 6 servings.

ONE-STEP CREAMED POTATOES

3 cups diced raw potatoes (3 or
4 medium potatoes)
1 cup milk
2 tablespoons butter or margarine
1 teaspoon salt
Dash pepper

Combine potatoes, milk, butter, salt, and pepper in a 2-quart saucepan. Simmer covered 15 to 20 minutes, or till potatoes are tender. Stir occasionally. Makes 4 to 6 servings.

SCALLOPED POTATOES

Dandy with pork chops—

2 medium onions, thinly sliced
and separated in rings
1 package dry instant scalloped
potato mix
1 tablespoon snipped parsley

Mix sliced onions, potatoes from mix, and parsley in a 10x6x1½-inch baking dish; continue preparing potatoes and baking as directed on package. Makes 6 servings.

CREAMY BROILED POTATOES

Good way to use leftover cooked potatoes—

4 medium potatoes, cooked
1 8-ounce carton French onion sour
   cream dip (1 cup)
1 8-ounce carton dairy sour cream
   (1 cup)
   Paprika

Dice potatoes (about 3 cups). Combine with onion dip and sour cream. Spread out on heat-proof platter. Place about 5 inches from heat and broil for 10 to 12 minutes. Sprinkle with paprika before serving. Makes 4 to 6 servings.

BARBECUE BEANS

Canned pork and beans with a real home cooked flavor—

2 1-pound cans (4 cups) pork and
   beans in tomato sauce
¾ cup brown sugar
1 teaspoon dry mustard
6 slices bacon, cut in small pieces
½ cup catsup

Empty 1 *can* of beans into a 1½-quart casserole. Combine brown sugar and mustard; sprinkle *half* of mixture over beans. Top with second can of beans; sprinkle with remaining brown sugar mixture, and the cut bacon. Spread catsup over all. Cover and bake in moderate oven (350°) 45 minutes. Makes 6 to 8 servings.

GREEN BEANS PLUS

A good way to glamorize canned beans—

1 cup sliced celery
2 tablespoons butter
1 teaspoon sugar
2 1-pound cans (4 cups) cut
   green beans

Cook the celery in the butter till crisp-tender; add sugar. Heat green beans; drain well. Toss lightly with celery and butter mixture. Season to taste with salt and pepper. Serves 6 to 8.

Deviled Green Beans have a tangy mustard flavor that you'll want to remember the next time you serve ham. Trim with parsley.

DEVILED GREEN BEANS

1 1-pound can cut green beans
1 tablespoon butter or margarine
2 teaspoons prepared mustard
½ teaspoon Worcestershire sauce
   Dash *each* salt and pepper
2 tablespoons corn flake crumbs

Heat beans; drain. In small saucepan, melt butter. Stir in remaining ingredients except crumbs. Pour over hot beans; stir gently. Sprinkle with corn flake crumbs. Serves 4.

BROCCOLI WITH EASY HOLLANDAISE

2 10-ounce packages frozen
   broccoli spears
½ cup dairy sour cream
½ cup mayonnaise or salad dressing
1 teaspoon prepared mustard
2 teaspoons lemon juice

Cook broccoli according to package directions. Meanwhile, combine remaining ingredients in saucepan. Cook and stir over low heat till just heated. Serve over broccoli. Serves 6 to 8.

CURRY-CREAMED ONIONS

  1 1-pound can (2 cups) whole onions
  1 10½-ounce can condensed cream
      of mushroom soup
  ⅓ cup milk
  ¼ teaspoon curry powder

Drain onions. In saucepan, blend soup, milk, and curry powder; add onions. Heat slowly, stirring once or twice, till bubbly and hot. Makes about 4 servings.

ONE-STEP CREAMED PEAS

Delicious way to cream any cooked vegetable, beginning with fresh, frozen, or canned—

  1 cup *cold* milk
  1 1-pound can (2 cups) peas,
      drained
  ½ teaspoon instant minced onion
  2 tablespoons instant-type flour
  ½ teaspoon salt
  ¼ teaspoon pepper
  2 tablespoons butter or margarine

Pour milk over peas; stir in remaining ingredients. Cook and stir over medium heat till mixture comes to boiling; boil 1 minute. Makes about 4 servings.

GARDEN PEAS—OVEN STYLE

Good to include in an oven meal—

  2 10-ounce packages frozen peas,
      thawed enough to separate*
  1 3-ounce can sliced mushrooms,
      drained (½ cup)
  ¼ cup chopped onion
  ¼ teaspoon salt
  ¼ teaspoon dried savory, crushed
      Dash pepper
  2 tablespoons butter or margarine
  1 tablespoon water

Combine all ingredients in a 1½-quart casserole. Cover and bake at 350° for 1 hour, or till tender. Stir once or twice. Serves 8.

  *To hasten thawing, pour boiling water over peas; drain thoroughly.

MINTED PEAS

  1 1-pound can (2 cups) peas
  ½ teaspoon salt
  ⅛ teaspoon pepper
  1 tablespoon butter or margarine
  ¼ cup mint-flavored jelly

Drain liquid from peas into a saucepan and cook till ¼ cup remains. Add peas, seasonings, butter or margarine, and jelly. Simmer to heat through and blend flavors. Serves 4.

SPECIAL SPINACH

  1 10-ounce package frozen chopped
      spinach
  1 cup small-curd, cream-style
      cottage cheese
  1 tablespoon *dry* onion soup mix

Cook spinach in ¼ cup water just till tender (do not salt the water); drain thoroughly, pressing out liquid.

  Stir in cottage cheese and onion soup mix. Cook over low heat, stirring occasionally, till mixture is hot. Makes 3 or 4 servings.

BROILED TOMATOES WITH DILL-SOUR CREAM SAUCE

Remember these tomatoes for broiler meals—

  ½ cup dairy sour cream
  ¼ cup mayonnaise or salad dressing
  2 tablespoons finely chopped onion
  ¼ teaspoon dried dillweed *or*
      1 teaspoon snipped fresh dill
  ¼ teaspoon salt
      • • •
  3 large firm ripe tomatoes
      Salt and pepper
      Butter or margarine

Combine sour cream, mayonnaise, onion, dill, and the ¼ teaspoon salt; mix well; chill. Core tomatoes and cut in half crosswise. Season cut surfaces with salt and pepper; dot with butter or margarine.

  Broil, cut side up, 3 inches from heat about 5 minutes or till heated through. Spoon sauce over broiled tomatoes. Makes 6 servings.

SQUASH WITH ONIONS

Rinse 2 acorn squash; cut in halves lengthwise; remove seeds. Place squash, cut side down, in shallow pan. Bake in a slow oven (325°) till almost tender, 45 to 50 minutes. Turn cut side up and sprinkle with salt; continue baking till tender, 15 minutes.

Heat one 9-ounce package frozen onions with cream sauce according to package directions. Spoon into squash centers. Sprinkle with paprika. Makes 4 servings.

VEGETABLE TOPPERS

Concoct toppers for vegetables such as:

• Toasted crisp walnuts as croutons, sauteed mushrooms or onions, or toasted sesame seed.
• Grated cheese, snipped chives, or crumbled crisp bacon.
• Pimiento strips or olive slices.
• Hard-cooked egg slices for sauced vegetables.
• Flavored butters like Tomato Topper, below.

TOMATO TOPPER

¼ cup finely chopped, seeded fresh
    tomato
Dash basil
Dash freshly ground pepper
½ cup butter or margarine, softened

Blend tomato, basil, and pepper with the butter or margarine. Serve on cooked green beans, cauliflower, broccoli, peas, or Lima beans. Refrigerate any extra topper.

VELVET CHEESE SAUCE

2 ounces sharp process American
    cheese, shredded (½ cup)
¼ cup mayonnaise or salad dressing
½ cup dairy sour cream
Paprika

Combine cheese and mayonnaise; cook and stir over low heat till cheese melts. Blend in sour cream; heat through. Dash with paprika. (For extra-smooth sauce, beat with rotary beater just before serving.) Makes 1 cup sauce.

Just shred 2 ounces sharp process American cheese directly onto the *hot* vegetable.

For a quick sauce, combine one 10½-ounce can condensed cream of mushroom soup and ⅓ cup milk; heat. Add 4 ounces sharp process American cheese, shredded (1 cup); stir to melt. Makes 1⅔ cups.

Cheese, mayonnaise, and sour cream are all you need to make Velvet Cheese Sauce.

SHORTCUT BREADS

PUMPKIN NUT BREAD

A mix, canned pumpkin, and spices make this delicious quick bread—

- ¾ cup canned pumpkin
- ½ cup water
- 1 egg
- 1 teaspoon ground cinnamon
- ½ teaspoon ground mace
- 1 1-pound 1-ounce package nut quick bread mix
  Golden Glaze

In mixing bowl, blend pumpkin, water, egg, and spices. Add dry nut bread mix; stir till moistened. Turn into 3 greased 5½x3x2-inch loaf pans (or one 9x5x3-inch loaf pan). Bake in a moderate oven (350°) for 35 to 40 minutes or till done (50 minutes for large loaf).

Frost with *Golden Glaze:* Combine 2 cups sifted confectioners' sugar, 2 tablespoons light cream, and a few drops yellow food coloring; spread on cooled pumpkin loaves. (Halve recipe to glaze one large loaf.) Garnish with walnuts and candy corn.

CHEESE-TOPPED BISCUITS

Serve with a seafood salad for lunch—

- 2 packages refrigerated biscuits (20 biscuits)
- 1 4-ounce package (1 cup) shredded sharp Cheddar cheese
- 2 tablespoons light cream
- ½ teaspoon poppy seed
  Dash dry mustard

Arrange 15 biscuits, overlapping, around outside edge of a well-greased 9x1½-inch round cake pan. Use remaining 5 biscuits to make inner circle of overlapping biscuits. Combine cheese, cream, poppy seed, and mustard; crumble evenly over top of biscuits. Bake in hot oven (425°) about 15 minutes. Remove from pan immediately. Serve hot. Serves 8 to 10.

LAZY DAISY COFFEE CAKE

- 2 packages refrigerated orange Danish rolls with icing (8 rolls)
  Shredded coconut, tinted yellow

Open packages of rolls; unwind rolls and separate in individual strips. Beginning at center of large ungreased baking sheet, wind 5 strips in large coil. For petals: Wind remaining 11 strips in *individual* coils; place around center coil, being sure open end is next to the center coil. Pinch other end to make petal tip (see picture). Bake in hot oven (400°) 10 to 12 minutes or till lightly browned. Drizzle with icing from package. Sprinkle petal edges and center with tinted coconut.

PINE-COT COFFEE CAKE

- ½ teaspoon grated orange peel
- 1 8-ounce package corn muffin mix
- 3 tablespoons pineapple-apricot preserves
- 3 tablespoons sugar
- 3 tablespoons all-purpose flour
- 2 tablespoons butter or margarine
- 3 tablespoons chopped nuts

Add orange peel to mix; prepare batter according to package directions. Pour into greased 8x1½-inch round pan. Dot preserves (cut any large pieces) evenly over batter.

Combine sugar and flour. Cut in butter till crumbly; stir in nuts. Sprinkle mixture evenly over batter. Bake coffee cake at 400° for 20 minutes, or till done. Serve warm in wedges. Makes 6 servings.

A trio of easily made breads

Quick breads as Pumpkin Nut Bread, → Cheese-topped Biscuits, and Lazy Daisy Coffee Cake will bring many compliments.

CHEESE BREAKFAST BISCUITS

    1 3-ounce package cream cheese,
        softened
    ¼ cup apricot preserves
    1 egg
    ½ teaspoon vanilla
         • • •
    1 package refrigerated biscuits
        (10 biscuits)
    ¼ cup chopped pecans

Beat together the first 4 ingredients. Flatten biscuits on ungreased baking sheet to about 3½-inch circles, building up rim on sides of each. Place about 1 tablespoon filling in center of each. Sprinkle nuts over filled rolls. Bake in moderate oven (375°) for 14 to 16 minutes. Serve warm. Makes 10 biscuits.

ALMOND CRESCENT ROLLS

Unroll and separate 1 package refrigerated crescent rolls (8 rolls). Using one half 12-ounce can almond filling (½ cup), spread 1 tablespoon almond filling on each unrolled crescent. Roll up and bake according to package directions. Serve warm. Makes 8 crescents.

QUICK APPLE PINWHEEL

    1 package refrigerated
        crescent rolls (8 rolls)
         • • •
    1 medium apple, cored, pared, and
        chopped (about 1 cup)
    ¼ cup raisins
    2 tablespoons sugar
    ½ teaspoon grated lemon peel
        Dash ground nutmeg

Unroll and separate crescent rolls. On greased baking sheet, arrange triangles in complete circle, bases overlapping at center and points toward outside. (Leave center of circle open.)

For filling, combine remaining ingredients; spoon over bases of triangles. Fold points over filling, tucking points under bases of triangles at center circle. Brush with a little milk; sprinkle with 1 tablespoon brown sugar. Bake in moderate oven (350°) for 25 minutes or till golden brown. Makes 1 coffee cake.

STICKY BUNS

    2 tablespoons butter or margarine
    ¼ cup brown sugar
    2 teaspoons light corn syrup
    ¼ cup broken pecan halves
    1 package refrigerated biscuits
        (10 biscuits)

Melt butter in 8x1½-inch round pan. Add brown sugar and corn syrup; heat till sugar dissolves. Scatter pecans on bottom. Place biscuits atop in single layer.

Bake in hot oven (425°) about 15 minutes or till done. Let stand 5 minutes. Invert and serve warm. Makes 10 buns.

JIFFY DOUGHNUTS

Stretch and flatten slightly each biscuit from a package of refrigerated biscuits (10 biscuits). With finger, punch hole in center and shape in doughnut. Fry in deep hot fat (375°) about 2 minutes, turning once. Drain on paper toweling. Roll in mixture of cinnamon and sugar. Serve warm. Makes 10 doughnuts.

QUICK BISMARCKS

Luscious jelly-filled treats for breakfast or dessert. Coffee is a must—

Flatten each biscuit from a package of refrigerated biscuits (10 biscuits) to ¼ inch. Place 1 teaspoon jam or jelly on *half* the biscuits; cover with remaining biscuits; seal edges well. Fry in deep hot fat (375°) about 3 minutes on each side.

Drain on paper toweling. Dust with confectioners' sugar. Serve warm. Makes 5.

QUICKY CRULLERS

Carefully unroll one package refrigerated crescent rolls (8 rolls). Pinch together diagonal perforations of each 2 crescents, making 4 rectangles. Cut in thirds lengthwise, and tie each strip in knot. Fry in deep hot fat (375°) till browned. Drain on paper toweling. While warm, glaze with confectioners' sugar glaze. Makes 12 crullers.

ORANGE DANISH BRAID

Remove rolls from 1 package refrigerated orange Danish rolls with icing (8 rolls) and unroll into long strips. Loosely braid 3 strips together; place on ungreased baking sheet. Repeat with 3 strips; place on sheet next to first braid. Twist remaining 2 strips together; place on top of braids. Bake at 400° for 15 to 18 minutes. Combine icing and one 3-ounce package cream cheese, softened; spread over warm braid. Sprinkle with 2 tablespoons chopped pecans and 1 tablespoon chopped maraschino cherries, well drained. Serves 6.

PEACH COFFEE CAKE

    1 14-ounce package orange muffin
       mix
    1 1-pound can sliced peaches,
       drained
    ½ cup brown sugar
    ⅓ cup all-purpose flour
    ½ teaspoon ground cinnamon
    ¼ cup butter or margarine

Prepare muffin mix according to package directions. Spread in a greased 9x9x2-inch baking pan. Arrange peach slices in rows atop.

Combine brown sugar, flour, and cinnamon. Cut in butter or margarine till mixture is crumbly. Sprinkle over top. Bake at 400° for 25 minutes, or till done. Serves 6 to 8.

PINEAPPLE-ORANGE MUFFINS

    1 14-ounce package orange muffin
       mix
    ½ cup flaked coconut
    1 8¾-ounce can crushed pineapple
    1 beaten egg
    ⅔ cup milk
    1 3-ounce package cream cheese

Combine muffin mix and coconut. Drain pineapple, reserving 1 tablespoon syrup. Add pineapple, egg, and milk to dry ingredients; blend only till dry ingredients are moistened. Fill greased muffin pans ⅔ full. Bake at 400° for 15 to 20 minutes, or till done. Beat cream cheese till fluffy. Add reserved pineapple syrup. Serve with hot muffins. Makes 12 to 16.

POPPY ONION LOAF

    ¼ cup butter or margarine
    1 tablespoon poppy seed
    1 tablespoon instant minced onion
    2 packages refrigerated butterflake
       rolls (24 rolls)

Melt butter or margarine; add poppy seed and onion. Separate each dinner roll into 2 or 3 pieces. Spread butter mixture between each. Place each piece on edge in a 9x5x3-inch loaf pan, arranging them in two rows.

Bake in a moderate oven (375°) for 20 to 25 minutes, or till golden brown. Turn out onto plate. Makes 6 to 8 servings.

CHEESE BISCUIT LOAF

    1 package refrigerated
       biscuits (10 biscuits)
    2 tablespoons butter or margarine,
       melted
    ¼ cup grated Parmesan cheese

Dip biscuits in melted butter, then in cheese. Arrange in 2 overlapping rows on baking sheet. Bake in a very hot oven (475°) 8 to 10 minutes. Makes 5 or 6 servings.

BANANA COFFEE CAKE

Fragrant banana bread in quick coffee-cake form is a tasty addition to breakfast—

    1 small ripe banana
    1 10½-ounce package coffee cake mix
    ½ cup milk
    1 egg
    ¼ cup chopped walnuts

On cutting board, mash banana slightly with a fork. (Small banana will yield about ⅓ cup.) Prepare coffee cake mix according to package directions, adding mashed banana with milk and egg. Pour batter into foil pan provided in package.

Sprinkle coffee cake batter with topping provided in mix package. Top with chopped walnuts. Bake in moderate oven (375°) for 25 to 30 minutes. Makes 1 coffee cake or 6 to 8 servings.

QUICK SWEDISH RYE BREAD

1 13¾-ounce package hot roll mix
2 eggs

• • •

¾ cup medium rye flour
1 tablespoon brown sugar
2 tablespoons molasses
1 to 2 teaspoons caraway seed

Prepare hot roll mix according to package directions, *using 2 eggs.* Stir in rye flour, brown sugar, molasses, and caraway seed. Let rise according to package directions. Turn out on floured surface, tossing lightly to cover dough with flour. Divide dough in half; shape in loaves. Place in two greased 8½x4½x2½-inch baking dishes. Let rise according to package directions. Bake in a moderate oven (350°) about 30 minutes. Makes 2 loaves.

DEVILED HAM BITS

Stir one 4½-ounce can deviled ham, 2 teaspoons prepared horseradish, and 2 or 3 dashes bottled hot pepper sauce into ¼ cup melted butter or margarine. Spread *half* the mixture in 9x9x2-inch baking pan.

Top with one package refrigerated biscuits (10 biscuits), quartered. Spoon remaining ham mixture over biscuits. Bake in hot oven (400°) for 12 to 15 minutes. Serve warm with picks as appetizers. Makes 40.

CRESCENT ROLL-UPS

1 package refrigerated crescent rolls (8 rolls)
½ cup dairy sour cream
½ teaspoon onion salt
½ pound bacon, crisp-cooked, drained, and crumbled

Unroll and separate crescent rolls; spread with sour cream and sprinkle with onion salt. Top with crumbled bacon. Cut each roll lengthwise into 3 equal wedges, roll up each, starting at the point of the wedge.

Place roll-ups on greased baking sheet; bake in moderate oven (375°) for 12 to 15 minutes, or till golden brown. Serve warm as appetizers. Makes 2 dozen.

HONEY CRUNCH LOAF

1 round loaf unsliced white bread
½ cup butter or margarine, melted
½ cup honey
½ cup sugar-coated cereal
½ cup flaked coconut
½ cup brown sugar

Slice bread *almost* to the bottom, 4 or 5 times in each direction. Place loaf on piece of foil on baking sheet; turn up edges of foil. Combine the butter or margarine with ¼ *cup of the honey;* spoon over top of loaf and let excess drizzle between the sections. Combine cereal, coconut, and brown sugar; sprinkle on top of loaf and between sections. Drizzle with the remaining ¼ cup honey. Heat at 350° for 20 minutes or till lightly browned.

HERB BUTTERED BREAD

1½ teaspoons snipped chives
1½ teaspoons snipped parsley
¼ teaspoon dried tarragon, crushed
¼ teaspoon dried chervil, crushed
¼ cup butter, softened
8 slices French bread

Mix together first 5 ingredients. Spread on French bread slices. Place on baking sheet and bake in moderate oven (350°) till lightly toasted, about 20 minutes. Serve warm.

SCALLION BUTTERED ROLLS

Blend ½ cup butter, 1 tablespoon finely chopped scallions (green onions), 1 tablespoon finely snipped parsley, and ¼ to ½ teaspoon dried rosemary, crushed. Halve 6 hard rolls; spread with butter mixture. Wrap in foil; heat on grill or in oven 10 minutes, or till hot.

POPPY SEED ROLLS

In foilware pan, melt 3 tablespoons butter. Add 1 teaspoon poppy seed and 2 tablespoons grated Parmesan cheese. Section 6 brown and serve cloverleaf rolls; arrange in mixture in pan. Brown on grill or in moderate oven, turning till all sides of rolls are toasted.

CHEESE CORN BREAD

⅔ cup milk
1 teaspoon prepared mustard
1 well beaten egg

• • •

1 14-ounce package corn muffin mix
½ cup shredded Parmesan cheese
2 ounces sharp natural Cheddar
cheese, shredded (½ cup)

Blend milk and mustard and add beaten egg. Combine corn muffin mix and Parmesan cheese. Add milk mixture, stirring till just mixed. Pour into 8x8x2-inch baking pan. Bake in a hot oven (400°) for 18 to 20 minutes.

Sprinkle Cheddar cheese evenly over the top and bake 1 minute longer or until cheese is slightly melted. Serve warm. Serves 8 or 9.

BACON CHIVE CORN MUFFINS

1 14-ounce package corn muffin mix
2 teaspoons snipped chives
Dash pepper
6 slices bacon, crisp-cooked, drained,
and crumbled

Prepare muffin mix according to package directions. Fold in chives, pepper, and bacon. Turn into 12 greased 2¾-inch muffin pans and bake at 400° for 15 to 17 minutes or till done. Serve hot. Makes 12.

CORN AND CORN MUFFINS

Two versions of corn make these muffins doubly good—

1 14-ounce package corn muffin mix
1 8¾-ounce can (about 1 cup)
cream-style corn
1 beaten egg
2 ounces sharp process American
cheese, shredded (½ cup)
Dash bottled hot pepper sauce

Combine all ingredients in a large mixing bowl. Stir till blended. Fill large greased muffin pans ⅔ full. Bake in a hot oven (425°) 12 to 15 minutes or till muffins are brown. Makes 10 to 12 large muffins.

POTATO PANCAKES

4 eggs
⅔ cup sifted all-purpose flour
1½ teaspoons salt
2 tablespoons salad oil
½ cup milk
½ small onion
2 cups diced pared raw potatoes
(about ¾ pound)
1 teaspoon color keeper

Put eggs in blender container; cover and blend till fluffy, about 5 seconds. Add remaining ingredients in order given and blend about 5 seconds, or till potatoes are finely grated—not lumpy. Bake on hot, greased griddle about 2 minutes on each side, using about 2 tablespoons batter for each. Turn once. Do not stack pancakes. Serve with hot applesauce. Makes about 2½ dozen pancakes.

APPLE-SAUCED POTATOCAKES

Prepare one 3-ounce envelope potato pancake mix according to package directions. Add 1 cup chopped canned luncheon meat. For each pancake, drop about 2 tablespoons batter on hot, greased griddle. Bake. Serve with warm applesauce dashed with ground cinnamon. Makes about 10 to 12 small pancakes.

QUICK CHEESE PANCAKES

1½ cups milk
1 egg
¾ cup cream-style cottage cheese
1½ cups packaged pancake mix
2 tablespoons butter or margarine,
melted
1 teaspoon shredded orange peel

Place milk, egg, and cottage cheese in blender container; cover container and switch blender on and off 3 or 4 times, till cottage cheese is in small pieces. (Or beat with mixer.) Pour into a bowl. Add pancake mix; stir just till moistened. Stir in butter or margarine and shredded orange peel.

Bake on hot, lightly greased griddle, using ¼ cup batter for each. Serve with fresh orange slices and coconut. Makes 12 pancakes.

HEARTY SANDWICHES

TUNA TUGS

Perky and colorful luncheon treat—

1 6½- or 7-ounce can tuna, drained
1 tablespoon lemon juice
2 hard-cooked eggs, coarsely chopped
¼ cup sliced sweet pickle
2 tablespoons sliced green onion
¼ teaspoon salt
Dash pepper
3 English muffins, split, toasted, and spread with butter
Boston or Bibb lettuce
3 medium tomatoes, thinly sliced
½ cup mayonnaise or salad dressing

Break tuna in chunks and sprinkle with lemon juice; combine with hard-cooked eggs, pickle, onion, salt, and pepper. Mix gently and chill. Top each English muffin half with Boston lettuce, 3 tomato slices, and tuna salad. Garnish with a dollop of mayonnaise. Serves 6.

CORNED BEEF CAPTAINS

1 pint coleslaw
2 teaspoons prepared mustard
4 slices whole wheat bread, toasted and spread with butter
1 12-ounce can corned beef, chilled and sliced (8 slices)

Blend coleslaw and mustard. Spoon coleslaw mixture onto toast slices and arrange 2 slices of corned beef on top of each sandwich. Garnish with skewered cherry tomato and green onion. Makes 4 servings.

Three open-face salad sandwiches

← Tuna Tugs, Corned Beef Captains, and Chef's Salad in a Roll—a trio of knife and fork sandwiches—easy on the waistline.

CHEF'S SALAD IN A ROLL

4 French rolls
Butter or margarine, softened
• • •
Romaine
4 ounces sharp process American cheese, cut in julienne strips
4 slices pressed ham
4 slices salami
2 hard-cooked eggs, sliced
French salad dressing

Split rolls lengthwise, cutting *to but not through* crust at back. Spread cut surfaces with butter or margarine. For each sandwich: Cover bottom half of roll with romaine, then with cheese strips, and a fold-over of pressed ham and salami. Place egg slices atop foldovers. Drizzle each sandwich with about 1 tablespoon French dressing. Anchor tops with wooden picks, if needed. Makes 4 servings.

FOUR-STAR SANDWICH

12 slices bacon
6 tomato slices, ½ inch thick
• • •
1 11-ounce can condensed Cheddar cheese soup
¼ cup light cream
6 slices toast, spread with butter
1 cup cooked cauliflower

Arrange bacon strips on rack in shallow pan, with fat edge of each strip slightly overlapping lean of next strip. Bake in hot oven (400°) 12 to 15 minutes, or till of desired crispness. Ten minutes before bacon is done, add tomato slices to rack.

Meanwhile, in saucepan combine soup and cream; heat through. To assemble sandwiches: Top each slice of toast with a hot tomato slice, a few pieces of cauliflower, and some of the cheese sauce. Arrange 2 strips of bacon, crisscross fashion, on each sandwich. Serve hot. Makes 6 open-face sandwiches.

DILLED SALMON-WICH

Combine one 7¾-ounce can salmon, flaked, ⅓ cup dairy sour cream*, ½ teaspoon lemon juice, ¼ teaspoon dried dillweed, ¼ teaspoon salt, and ¼ cup chopped pecans. Chill.

Butter 8 slices white bread; spread about ¼ cup filling on 4 slices; place lettuce leaf on each. Top with second buttered slice of bread. Hold together with wooden pick topped with ripe olive garnish. Makes 4 servings.

*For a more moist filling, add an additional 2 tablespoons dairy sour cream.

SCANDINAVIAN SANDWICH

    4 English muffins
      Butter or margarine
      Prepared mustard
    8 slices salami *or* bologna
              • • •
    1 1-pound can (2 cups) French-style
      green beans, well drained
    2 tomatoes, sliced
    1 8-ounce package sliced sharp process
      American cheese (8 slices)

Split muffins; toast and spread with butter and mustard. Place on each muffin half: 1 salami slice, about ¼ cup well-drained beans, and 1 tomato slice. Broil 5 to 6 inches from heat for about 10 minutes or till hot. Top with cheese slice; broil till cheese begins to melt. Serve immediately. Serves 8.

FRANK-REUBEN SANDWICH

    8 frankfurters
    1 1-pound can sauerkraut, drained
      and snipped
    4 slices process Swiss cheese,
      quartered in strips
    8 frankfurter buns
      Thousand Island Dressing

Slit frankfurters in half lengthwise. Spread with sauerkraut. Broil 3 to 4 inches from heat for about 5 minutes or till sauerkraut is hot. Top with 2 cheese strips. Broil till cheese is melted. Toast buns; spread with Thousand Island Dressing. Serve frankfurters on buns. Makes 8 sandwiches.

SWISS YODELERS

    8 ounces process Swiss cheese,
      shredded (2 cups)
    ½ cup whipping cream
              • • •
    12 slices white bread
     9 slices bacon, cooked and drained
     1 3-ounce can chopped mushrooms,
       drained (½ cup)
              • • •
    ½ cup milk
    3 slightly beaten eggs
      Butter or margarine

Mix together cheese and cream. Spread 2 tablespoons mixture on each of *half* the bread slices. Halve cooked bacon slices. Place bacon pieces and drained mushrooms on top of cheese. Top with remaining bread.

Combine milk and eggs. Dip sandwiches in milk-egg mixture, coating both sides. Lightly brown sandwiches in melted butter on grill, turning once. Garnish with bacon curls and mushrooms, if desired. Makes 6 sandwiches.

BLUE CHEESE BURGERS

    1½ pounds ground beef
     1 slightly beaten egg
     1 teaspoon salt
     ¼ teaspoon pepper
     4 ounces blue cheese, crumbled
       (1 cup)
     1 teaspoon dry mustard
     2 tablespoons mayonnaise or salad
       dressing
     2 tablespoons Worcestershire sauce
              • • •
     4 hamburger buns, split and toasted

Thoroughly mix beef, egg, salt, and pepper; divide in 8 mounds. Flatten each to ½ inch patty between squares of waxed paper.

For filling, blend blue cheese with next 3 ingredients. Top *half* the meat patties with blue-cheese filling (leave ½-inch margin for sealing). Cover filling with remaining patties as "lids," sealing the edges well.

Broil 4 inches from heat, about 5 minutes on first side. Turn, broil 5 minutes more or till done to your liking. Slip patties into hot toasted buns. Makes 4 burgers.

Franks are topped with a savory combination of canned chili, cheese soup, and instant minced onion. Serve Chili-cheese Franks with celery sticks and ripe olives.

CHILI-CHEESE FRANKS

An appetite-pleaser for hungry youngsters—

    2 15-ounce cans chili with beans
    1 11-ounce can condensed Cheddar
       cheese soup
    2 tablespoons instant minced onion
    1 pound frankfurters (8 to 10)
    8 to 10 frankfurter buns, split
       and toasted
       Corn chips, coarsely crushed

In large saucepan, combine chili with beans, cheese soup, and onion. Add frankfurters; heat to boiling. Simmer mixture about 5 minutes to blend flavors.

To serve, place a frankfurter on each toasted frankfurter bun; top each with chili-cheese sauce and sprinkle with crushed corn chips. Makes 8 to 10 sandwiches.

BLUE CHEESE DOGS

Robust cheese makes hot dogs really special—

    ⅓ cup dairy sour cream
    2 tablespoons instant minced onion
    ¼ cup sweet pickle relish
    2 tablespoons prepared mustard
    ¼ cup crumbled blue cheese
        • • •
    8 frankfurter buns, split and
       toasted
    8 frankfurters

Combine sour cream, onion, pickle relish, mustard, and blue cheese. Spread 2 tablespoons cheese mixture on inside of each bun; insert a frankfurter. Wrap buns in heavy foil; heat in hot oven (400°) or on grill over medium coals for 10 minutes or till heated through. Makes 8 servings.

SOUP FIX UPS

Crab Bisque is as simple as "open the cans and heat" with a gourmet touch of wine. It's a real flavor treat requiring little effort.

CRAB BISQUE

    1 10½-ounce can condensed cream of
       asparagus soup
    1 10½-ounce can condensed cream of
       mushroom soup
    2 soup cans milk
    1 cup light cream
    1 7½-ounce can crab meat, drained,
       flaked, and cartilage removed
    ⅓ cup sherry

Blend soups; gradually stir in milk and cream. Heat just to boiling. Add crab meat; heat through. Just before serving, stir in sherry. Float butter atop. Sprinkle with snipped parsley. Makes 6 to 8 servings.

CHEESE BISQUE

    To one 11-ounce can condensed Cheddar cheese soup, add 1 cup light cream and ⅓ cup sherry. Heat and stir. Serves 3 or 4.

TUNA CHOWDER

    1 4-ounce envelope *dry* green pea
       soup mix
    ⅓ cup packaged precooked rice
    2 teaspoons instant minced onion
    3 cups cold water
    1 6½- or 7-ounce can tuna, drained
       Salt and pepper

In saucepan, combine green pea soup mix, rice, and instant minced onion; stir in the cold water. Cook, stirring frequently, till mixture is boiling. Cover; simmer 3 minutes. Stir in tuna; add salt and pepper to taste. Cook till heated through. Makes 4 servings.

SHRIMP CHOWDER

    ½ cup finely chopped onion
    1 tablespoon butter or margarine
    1 10½-ounce can condensed cream of
       celery soup
    1 10¾-ounce can condensed clam
       chowder
    1½ soup cans water
    1 4½-ounce can shrimp, drained
    1 tablespoon snipped parsley

In saucepan, cook onion in butter till tender. Blend in remaining ingredients. Simmer about 5 minutes, till flavors blend. Serves 6.

POTATO PEA POTAGE

    1 10½-ounce can frozen condensed
       green pea with ham soup
    1 10¼-ounce can frozen condensed
       cream of potato soup
    1½ soup cans water
    4 ounces sharp process American
       cheese, shredded (1 cup)

In saucepan, combine soups, water, and cheese. Heat, stirring occasionally. Serves 4.

QUICK CLAM CHOWDER

1 7½-ounce can minced clams
¼ cup chopped celery
1 teaspoon instant minced onion
1 tablespoon butter or margarine
1 8-ounce package frozen green peas
  and potatoes with cream sauce
1 13¾-ounce can condensed chicken
  broth
1 6-ounce can (⅔ cup) evaporated
  milk
¼ teaspoon thyme
  Paprika

Drain clams, reserving liquid. Cook celery and onion in the butter or margarine till tender, but not brown. Stir in peas and potatoes with cream sauce, chicken broth, evaporated milk, clam liquid, thyme, dash salt, and dash pepper. Cook and stir till mixture is boiling. Reduce heat; cover and simmer about 5 minutes. Stir in clams; heat to boiling. Garnish with paprika. Serves 4 to 6.

ITALIAN NOODLE SOUP

1 10½-ounce can condensed beef
  broth
1 1-pound can tomatoes
½ cup water
1 cup (1¼ ounces) fine egg noodles
¼ teaspoon dried basil, crushed
  Dash pepper
  Grated Parmesan cheese

Combine ingredients except cheese in a saucepan, breaking up tomatoes. Cook, uncovered, over medium heat 8 to 10 minutes, or till noodles are tender, stirring occasionally. Pass grated Parmesan cheese. Makes 4 servings.

TOMATO CHICKEN-RICE SOUP

2 10¾-ounce cans condensed tomato
  soup
1 10½-ounce can condensed chicken-
  rice soup
1½ soup cans milk

Combine all ingredients in saucepan. Cook and stir till heated through. Serves 4 or 5.

DEVIL'S CHOWDER

1 10½-ounce can condensed cream
  of celery soup
1 8¾-ounce can cream-style corn
1 2¼-ounce can deviled ham
1 tablespoon instant minced onion
  Dash paprika
  Dash ground nutmeg
1 soup can milk

Combine celery soup, cream style corn, deviled ham, instant minced onion, paprika, and nutmeg in saucepan. Gradually stir in the milk. Cook and stir till heated through. Makes 2 or 3 servings.

CURRIED CHICKEN SOUP

Combine one 10½-ounce can condensed cream of chicken soup, 1 soup can milk, and ½ teaspoon curry powder. Mix well. Chill several hours. Just before serving, stir in 2 tablespoons snipped parsley. Pour into well-chilled bowls. Garnish with a sprig of parsley, if desired. Makes 3 or 4 servings.

CHILI FRANK SOUP

Cook 1 cup chopped carrots and ½ cup chopped celery in 1½ cups water and ¼ teaspoon salt till tender, 10 to 12 minutes. Add 4 frankfurters, sliced, one 11½-ounce can condensed bean with bacon soup, and one 11-ounce can condensed chili beef soup. Heat through, about 10 minutes. Makes 4 servings.

PEANUT BUTTER BISQUE

2 tablespoons finely chopped onion
1 tablespoon butter or margarine
¼ cup peanut butter
1 10½-ounce can condensed cream of
  chicken soup
1 soup can water
¼ cup milk

In saucepan, cook onion in butter till tender, but not brown. Blend in peanut butter. Add soup, water, and milk. Heat, stirring occasionally. Garnish with minced parsley. Serves 3.

TIMESAVING DESSERTS

ANGEL BERRY CAKE

    1 10-inch angel cake
    1 pint fresh raspberries, crushed
      and sweetened with ½ cup sugar
      or 1 10-ounce package frozen
      raspberries, thawed
    2 cups whipping cream
    ¼ cup sugar
    1 teaspoon vanilla
    6 drops red food coloring

With sharp, thin-bladed knife, make slits at
1-inch intervals around top of cake, between
center and rim, cutting through cake from top
to bottom. With knife, insert berries into slits.
Spoon juice evenly over berries. Whip cream
with sugar, vanilla, and food coloring. Frost
entire cake. Refrigerate 2 to 3 hours. Makes
8 to 10 servings.

ALMOND CHOCOLATE CAKE

    2 tablespoons butter, softened
    ½ cup sliced almonds
    2 tablespoons sugar
    1 package 2-layer-size
      chocolate cake mix

Grease a 10-inch tube pan including center
tube ¾ of the way up side, using 2 tablespoons
butter. Press sliced almonds into butter; sprinkle with sugar. Prepare cake mix according to
package directions. Carefully spoon over nuts.
Place baking sheet on bottom rack of oven:
Bake at 350° about 55 to 60 minutes, or till
cake tests done. Remove from oven and cool
10 minutes. Remove from pan and cool completely. Slice and serve topped with whipped
cream or ice cream.

Sweet red raspberries take a bow

← Serve a group with this pink dream—Angel
Berry Cake. It starts with an angel cake
from the bakery or one made from a mix.

APRICOT COCONUT RING

As shown opposite the contents page—

    1 1-pound 14-ounce can apricot
      halves
    3 tablespoons butter or margarine
    ⅓ cup brown sugar
    ⅔ cup flaked coconut
    1 package 1-layer-size white cake
      mix
    1 tablespoon cornstarch
    2 tablespoons brown sugar

Drain apricots, reserving syrup. Combine butter, 3 tablespoons reserved syrup, and ⅓ cup
brown sugar. Heat till butter melts and sugar
dissolves. Pour into a greased 5-cup ring mold
Sprinkle coconut evenly over.

  Prepare cake mix according to package directions; spoon over coconut. Bake at 350° for
25 to 30 minutes, or till done. Cool 1 minute;
invert on plate. Remove ring mold. Pile apricots in center.

  For glaze, mix cornstarch and 2 tablespoons
brown sugar in saucepan. Add remaining apricot syrup. Bring to boil. Cook till mixture is
thickened. Spoon glaze over sides and top of
cake and fruit. Makes 6 to 8 servings.

PINEAPPLE CRUNCH CAKE

    1 package 1-layer-size yellow cake
      mix
    1 8¾-ounce can crushed pineapple,
      well drained
        • • •
    ½ cup flaked coconut
    ⅓ cup brown sugar
    ⅓ cup chopped pecans
    3 tablespoons butter, melted

Prepare mix according to package directions.
Pour *half* the batter into a greased 8x8x2-inch
baking pan. Spoon pineapple over. Top with
remaining batter. Combine remaining ingredients. Spread over batter. Bake at 350° for
30 to 35 minutes. Serve warm. Serves 9.

APPLE-GINGERBREAD

A family favorite—now quickly prepared from foods easily stored in the kitchen cabinet—

Combine one 8½-ounce can applesauce with ¼ cup sugar, ¼ teaspoon ground mace, ¼ teaspoon shredded lemon peel, and dash salt. Prepare *half* of a 2-ounce package (⅓ cup) dessert topping mix according to package directions for that amount. Fold into applesauce mixture. Chill.

Prepare and bake 1 package gingerbread mix according to package directions. Cut in squares while still warm. Spoon chilled topper over gingerbread squares. Garnish with snipped candied ginger. Makes 6 to 8 servings.

BUTTERSCOTCH SPICE BAKE

Prepare one 4-ounce package *regular* butterscotch pudding mix according to package directions, *using 2¼ cups milk*. Blend into the hot pudding 1 package 2-layer-size spice cake mix (dry); mixture will not be smooth. Pour into lightly greased and floured 13x9x2-inch baking pan. Scatter ½ cup chopped walnuts over batter. Bake at 375° for 25 to 30 minutes. Cut in squares; serve warm or cold with whipped cream or ice cream. Serves 12 to 15.

PEANUT BUTTER PEACH CAKE

  ¼ cup butter or margarine
  ⅓ cup peanut butter
  ½ cup brown sugar
  1 1-pound can sliced peaches,
    drained (reserve ¼ cup syrup)
  1 package 1-layer-size yellow
    cake mix

In a saucepan, combine butter, peanut butter, brown sugar, and reserved peach syrup. Cook over medium heat till ingredients are melted and blended. Pour into an 8x8x2-inch baking pan. Place peaches in rows over mixture.

Prepare cake mix according to package directions. Carefully pour over top of peaches. Bake in a moderate oven (350°) about 50 minutes or till cake is done. Cool cake 5 minutes. Invert on cake plate. Serve plain or with whipped cream. Makes 9 servings.

ORANGE BABAS

  1 package 1-layer-size yellow cake
    mix
  ⅓ cup frozen orange juice
    concentrate, thawed
  ½ cup sugar
  ½ cup water

Prepare cake mix according to package directions. Turn batter into 8 well greased 5-ounce custard cups. Bake in moderate oven (350°) for 25 minutes. Let cool 5 minutes; remove to serving plate and drizzle with hot Orange Syrup. Cool. Serve with whipped cream, if desired. Garnish with sliced almonds. Serves 8.

For Orange Syrup, combine orange juice concentrate, sugar, and water. Bring to rolling boil; remove from heat.

MOCHA-VELVET TORTE

  1 12-ounce loaf pound cake
  1 4¼- or 4½-ounce package *instant* chocolate pudding mix
  1 tablespoon instant coffee powder
  1 2-ounce package dessert topping mix
  1¼ cups cold milk

Slice cake horizontally in 4 layers. For frosting, combine pudding mix, instant coffee powder, dessert topping mix, and milk in mixing bowl. Beat till fluffy and of spreading consistency. Spread three layers of cake with frosting; stack together and top with fourth layer. Frost top and sides of cake. Chill. Serves 10.

BUTTERSCOTCH DESSERT

  1 4-ounce package *instant* butterscotch pudding mix
  1 cup cold milk
  ½ cup dairy sour cream
    • • •
  ¼ cup flaked coconut

Combine pudding mix, milk, and sour cream in small bowl. Beat till ingredients are well blended. Fold in coconut. Spoon into sherbet glasses. Chill till served. Top with additional flaked coconut, if desired. Serves 4.

Pots de Creme Chocolate is traditionally rich and chocolaty. Nothing could be easier or quicker than this simple combination of pudding mix and semisweet chocolate pieces.

POTS DE CREME CHOCOLATE

MAKE AHEAD RECIPE

2¼ cups milk
1 4-ounce package *regular* chocolate pudding mix
1 6-ounce package (1 cup) semisweet chocolate pieces
1 teaspoon vanilla
Pressurized dessert topping

Using the 2¼ cups milk, prepare pudding mix according to package directions. While pudding is hot, add semisweet chocolate pieces; stir till melted; cool. Add vanilla and beat till smooth. Spoon into pot de creme cups and chill. Before serving, garnish with pressurized dessert topping. Makes 6 servings.

LAZY GRASSHOPPER PARFAITS

MAKE AHEAD RECIPE

1 3¾-ounce package vanilla whipped dessert mix
2 tablespoons green creme de menthe
1 tablespoon white creme de cacao
½ cup chocolate-wafer crumbs (8 wafers)

Prepare dessert mix according to package directions. Fold in creme de menthe and creme de cacao. Chill about 30 minutes or till mixture mounds when spooned.

Layer in parfait glasses with chocolate crumbs, using about 1 tablespoon crumbs between each layer. Chill. Garnish with additional chocolate wafer crumbs. Serves 4.

JIFFY BUTTERSCOTCH TORTE

A real quickie! It starts with a package of fluffy white frosting mix—

  1 package fluffy white frosting
     mix (for a 2-layer cake)
  1 teaspoon vanilla
        • • •
  1 cup graham-cracker crumbs
     (12 crackers)
  1 6-ounce package (1 cup) butter-
     scotch pieces
  ½ cup flaked coconut
  ½ cup chopped pecans
     Whipped cream

Prepare frosting mix according to package directions; stir in vanilla. Fold in graham-cracker crumbs, butterscotch pieces, coconut, and pecans. Turn into greased 9-inch pie plate. Bake in moderate oven (350°) for 30 minutes, or till lightly browned. Cut in wedges. Serve warm or cool with unsweetened whipped cream. Makes 8 servings.

PEANUT CHOCOLATE PUDDING

  1 4-ounce package *regular*
     chocolate pudding mix
  ¼ cup peanut butter

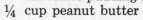

Prepare chocolate pudding according to package directions, *except use 2½ cups milk.* Immediately stir in the peanut butter. Turn into serving dishes. Chill. Before serving, garnish with whipped cream and chopped peanuts, if desired. Makes 4 servings.

CREME CARAMEL DESSERT

Interesting fix-up for packaged pudding mix—

  1 3- or 3¼-ounce package
     regular vanilla pudding mix
  2 tablespoons maple syrup

Prepare pudding according to package directions. Pour about 1½ *teaspoons* of the maple syrup into each of four 5-ounce custard cups. Carefully spoon in warm pudding. Chill till firm. Makes 4 servings.

FAST CREME BRULEE

  1 3- or 3¼-ounce package
     regular vanilla pudding mix
  ½ cup whipping cream, whipped
  ½ cup brown sugar

Prepare pudding according to package directions, *except use 1¾ cups milk.* Cool. Fold in whipped cream. Pour into 9-inch pie plate. Chill. Sprinkle brown sugar evenly over top. Place pie plate in shallow pan. Surround with ice cubes and a little cold water; broil about 5 inches from heat till bubbly brown crust forms, about 5 minutes. Chill. Serves 4 to 6.

BAKED APPLE BETTY

  1 1-pound 5-ounce can apple pie
     filling
  1 package 1-layer-size spice cake
     mix
  6 tablespoons butter or margarine,
     melted

Spread pie filling in buttered 9x9x2-inch baking pan. Sprinkle cake mix evenly over top of filling. Drizzle top with butter. Bake in a moderate oven (350°) for 40 to 45 minutes, or till top is golden brown. Serve warm with ice cream. Makes 6 servings.

CHERRY CHEESECAKE

  1 8-ounce package cream
     cheese, softened
  1 cup sifted confectioners' sugar
  1 teaspoon vanilla
  1 cup whipping cream, whipped
        • • •
  1 9-inch frozen pastry shell,
     baked
  ¼ teaspoon almond extract
  1 1-pound 5-ounce can cherry pie
     filling

Beat together cream cheese, confectioners' sugar, and vanilla till smooth. Fold in whipped cream. Pour into baked pastry shell. Add almond extract to cherry pie filling and carefully spoon over cheese layer. Chill till set, several hours or overnight. Makes 6 servings.

Classic Fruit-glazed Cheese Pie goes convenient in a grand style. Take honors with this pie and feel just a bit smug because it requires so little time and effort.

FRUIT-GLAZED CHEESE PIE

MAKE AHEAD · RECIPE ·

- 1 8-ounce package cream cheese, softened
- 1 cup dairy sour cream
- ½ cup sugar
- ½ teaspoon vanilla
- 1 9-inch graham-cracker crust or Vanilla Cookie Crust
- 1 16- or 17-ounce can or jar fruits for salad
- 5 tablespoons orange marmalade

Combine cream cheese, sour cream, sugar, and vanilla; beat till smooth. Pour into pie shell. Bake in moderate oven (375°) 20 minutes or till just set. Chill. Drain fruits thoroughly. Arrange in circle on chilled pie. Stir marmalade; spoon over fruits to glaze. Serves 6 to 8.

VANILLA COOKIE CRUST

Line bottom of buttered 9-inch pie plate with whole vanilla wafers. Trim ¼ inch off enough wafers to stand up-around edge of pie plate. Crumble a few wafers to fill in spaces in bottom crust.

PINEAPPLE PECAN PUDDING

Spoon this luscious dessert into dishes while still warm from the oven. Then let the ice cream melt over it—

- 1 1-pound 4½-ounce can (2½ cups) pineapple tidbits

• • •

- 1½ cups packaged biscuit mix
- ½ cup chopped pecans
- ⅓ cup milk

• • •

- ½ cup brown sugar
- 2 tablespoons butter or margarine
  Dash ground nutmeg
  Dash ground cinnamon

Drain pineapple, reserving syrup. Combine biscuit mix, drained pineapple tidbits, and pecans. Stir in milk. Spread batter in greased 10x6x1½-inch baking dish.

Add water to pineapple syrup to make 1½ cups. Combine with remaining ingredients in saucepan; bring to boiling. Pour evenly over batter. Bake in a moderate oven (375°) for 35 to 40 minutes. Serve warm with vanilla ice cream or cream. Makes 6 to 8 servings.

APRICOT-SCOTCH COBBLER

1 1-pound 5-ounce can apricot
   pie filling*
1 roll refrigerated butterscotch-
   nut cookie dough, sliced ¼
   inch thick
1 teaspoon sugar
   Dash ground cinnamon

Heat pie filling and pour into an 8-inch pie
plate. Slightly overlap cookie slices on top of
filling around edge of pie plate. (Bake any remaining cookies separately for snacks.) Sprinkle cookies on filling with a mixture of the
sugar and cinnamon. Bake at 350° about 25
minutes, or till cookies are done. Serve warm
or cold topped with ice cream. Serves 5.
   *Substitute any flavor pie filling as desired:
pineapple, peach, cherry, or blueberry.

INSTANT DATE APPLE TORTE

Spread one 1-pound 5-ounce can apple pie
filling in 9x9x2-inch baking pan. Sprinkle 1
teaspoon grated orange peel over; pour 2 tablespoons orange juice over all. Prepare date
filling from one 14-ounce package date bar
mix according to package directions. Stir in ½
cup chopped walnuts. Add crumbly mixture
from mix and 1 egg; blend. Spread over apples. Bake at 375° 35 to 40 minutes. Serve
with cream or ice cream. Serves 6

CINNAMON APPLE WHIRLS

1 1-pound 5-ounce can apple pie
   filling
½ cup fruit juice (orange, pineapple, or other)
2 tablespoons butter or margarine
⅓ cup chopped pecans
1 package refrigerated caramel
   nut rolls (8 rolls)
   Dairy sour cream

In a saucepan, combine pie filling, fruit juice,
butter, nuts, and topping mix from the caramel rolls. Bring to boiling. Pour into 11x7x
1½-inch baking pan. Top with caramel rolls.
Bake at 375° for 20 to 25 minutes. Serve warm
topped with sour cream. Serves 8.

CHOCOLATE-MINT PARFAITS

1 4¼- or 4½-ounce package
   instant chocolate pudding mix
½ teaspoon peppermint extract
4 or 5 drops red food coloring
3 tablespoons crushed peppermint
   candies
1 cup whipping cream, whipped
½ cup graham-cracker crumbs

Prepare pudding according to package directions. Cool. Add extract, food coloring, and
crushed candy to whipped cream. Spoon pudding, crumbs, and whipped cream in layers
into 6 parfait glasses. Repeat layers. Garnish
with additional candy. Chill. Serves 6.

FRUIT MEDLEY PARFAITS

1 3¾- or 3⅝-ounce package
   instant vanilla pudding mix
¼ cup cream sherry
1 cup whipping cream
1 tablespoon sugar
2 12-ounce packages frozen mixed
   fruit, partially thawed

Prepare pudding according to package directions, *using 1¾ cups milk*. Stir in sherry and
let stand 5 minutes. Whip cream and sugar together until stiff.
   Place peach slices from mixed fruit in bottom of chilled parfait glasses. Spoon pudding,
then whipped cream over fruit. Repeat twice,
using the other fruits. Top with whipped
cream and toasted sliced almonds, if desired.
Makes 4 to 6 servings.

CRAN-MINCE PARFAITS

1 3- or 3¼-ounce package
   regular vanilla pudding mix
1 cup whipping cream, whipped
1 cup prepared mincemeat, chilled
1 10-ounce package frozen cranberry-orange relish, thawed

Prepare pudding according to package directions; chill. Beat smooth; fold in whipped
cream. In 8 chilled parfait glasses, layer mincemeat, pudding, and relish. Serves 8.

CHOCOLATE NUT SUNDAE CUPS

1 3¾-ounce package chocolate
  fudge-flavored whipped dessert
  mix
¼ cup chopped pecans
1 jar butterscotch topping
⅓ cup broken pecans
  Vanilla ice cream

Prepare dessert mix with milk and water as
directed on package. Chill till almost set, 45
minutes to 1 hour. Stir; fold in the ¼ cup
chopped nuts. Drop onto waxed paper-lined
baking sheet in about ½ cup portions. Make
a depression in center of each with spoon to
make cups to hold a scoop of ice cream. Freeze
2 to 3 hours, or till firm.

Before serving, heat butterscotch topping
slightly. Stir in broken pecans. Place a scoop
of vanilla ice cream in each chocolate cup.
Top with warm butterscotch topping. If desired, garnish with pecan halves. Serves 4.

PINEAPPLE CHEESE PARFAITS

Tastes like cheesecake in a parfait glass—

1 2¾-ounce package vanilla
  custard mix (no-bake type)
2 cups milk

• • •

2 3-ounce packages cream cheese,
  softened
½ teaspoon vanilla
1 1-pound 5-ounce can
  pineapple pie filling

In saucepan, prepare custard according to
package directions using the milk. Remove
from heat. Gradually stir hot mixture into
cheese; mix well. Stir in vanilla. Chill custard
and pie filling till serving time. When ready
to serve, spoon alternate layers of mixture and
pie filling into parfait glasses. Top with additional pie filling if desired. Serves 6 to 8.

As scrumptious to eat as it looks

Assemble frozen Chocolate Nut Sundae
Cups at the last minute. For a variation,
try coffee ice cream for real mocha flavor.

EGGNOG BAVARIAN

- 2 envelopes (2 tablespoons)
  unflavored gelatin
- ½ cup cold water
- 1 quart (4 cups) dairy eggnog
  • • •
- 32 split ladyfingers or 16 whole

Soften gelatin in cold water. Add about 1 *cup* of the eggnog; heat and stir till gelatin is dissolved. Remove from heat and add remaining eggnog; mix well. Chill till partially set. Beat with electric or rotary beater till light and fluffy. If ladyfingers are whole, split lengthwise. Line bottom of 8-inch spring form pan, cutting to fit; line sides by standing ladyfingers on end all around. Pour in eggnog mixture. Chill firm. Serves 8 to 10.

BLENDER APPLESAUCE

- 4 medium apples, cored, pared,
  and cubed (about 4 cups)
- ¼ cup sugar
- ¼ cup water
- 2 tablespoons lemon juice
- 5 or 6 drops red food coloring

Put apples, sugar, water, lemon juice, and food coloring in blender container; cover and blend till smooth. Heat in saucepan over low heat to serve warm, or chill. Makes 2 cups.

PEACHES A LA RUM

- 3 tablespoons rum
- 1 1-pound 13-ounce can
  peach halves, drained
- 1 2-ounce package dessert topping
  mix
  Slivered toasted almonds

Drizzle 2 *tablespoons* rum over drained peach halves. Cover and chill for several hours. When ready to serve, prepare topping mix according to package directions. Stir in 1 tablespoon rum. Spoon some topping into 8 sherbet glasses. Top with peach half, rounded side down. Spoon additional topping in each peach cavity and sprinkle with slivered toasted almonds. Serve cold. Makes 8 servings.

Just toss flaked coconut with enough mint extract or creme-de-menthe syrup to suit your taste. Serve over fruit or sherbet.

BANANAS FLAMBE SUPREME

- 4 bananas, peeled and quartered
- 2 10-ounce packages frozen strawberries, thawed
- 1 tablespoon rum
- 3 tablespoons brandy (cognac)

Place bananas in 10x6x1½-inch baking dish. Pour strawberries over. Combine rum and 1 *tablespoon* brandy; drizzle evenly over berries; bake at 375° for 15 minutes. Heat remaining 2 tablespoons brandy; ignite and pour over fruit mixture. Serve immediately. Serves 6.

CREAM TOPPED PEARS

Blend ½ cup dairy sour cream and 1 to 2 tablespoons grenadine syrup. Spoon over 8 chilled canned pear halves. Serves 4.

CREAMY MANDARIN PEARS

½ pint vanilla ice cream
　Few drops to ¼ teaspoon rum
　　flavoring
　　　• • •
1 11-ounce can chilled mandarin
　oranges, drained
4 chilled canned pear halves

Stir ice cream to soften; mix with flavoring to taste. Arrange mandarin oranges over pear halves in dessert dishes. Spoon softened ice cream over top. Makes 4 servings.

SPICED APPLE PARFAITS

1 1-pound can applesauce
2 tablespoons sugar
1 teaspoon ground cinnamon
1 teaspoon lemon juice
¼ teaspoon ground nutmeg
　　　• • •
　Vanilla ice cream

Combine ingredients except ice cream in a 1 quart saucepan. Cook over medium heat for 5 minutes, stirring occasionally. Cool. Layer the sauce with vanilla ice cream in parfait glasses. Makes 5 or 6 servings.

CANTALOUPE A LA MODE

½ cup sugar
1 tablespoon cornstarch
　Dash salt
½ cup water
　　　• • •
1 cup blueberries
1 tablespoon lemon juice
½ teaspoon shredded lemon peel
　　　• • •
　Vanilla ice cream
2 small cantaloupes, halved and
　seeds removed

Blend sugar, cornstarch, and salt in saucepan. Stir in water. Cook, stirring constantly, till mixture boils. Add blueberries. Return to boiling and boil 1 minute. Add lemon juice and peel. Serve warm over vanilla ice cream in cantaloupe halves. Makes 4 servings.

PEPPERMINT PATTY ALASKAS

3 egg whites
½ teaspoon vanilla
¼ teaspoon cream of tartar
　Dash salt
⅓ cup sugar
4 sponge cake dessert cups
4 1½-ounce chocolate-coated
　peppermint ice cream patties
2 tablespoons crushed peppermint
　candies

Bring egg whites to room temperature. Add vanilla, cream of tartar, and salt; beat to soft peaks. Gradually add sugar, beating till stiff peaks form.

Place sponge cake dessert cups on cutting board. Top each with an ice cream patty and completely cover with meringue, spreading it thicker over ice cream and thinner around cake, being careful to seal edges at bottom. Sprinkle meringue with crushed candies. Bake in extremely hot oven (500°) 2 to 3 minutes or till meringue is browned. Serve at once or freeze. Makes 4 servings.

PARTY SPUMONI

1 quart vanilla ice cream
½ cup toasted slivered almonds
1 1¾-ounce bar milk chocolate,
　chopped
¼ cup chopped maraschino cherries
¼ teaspoon shredded orange peel
¼ teaspoon shredded lemon peel
　Few drops anise flavoring

Stir ice cream to soften slightly. Stir in remaining ingredients. Line muffin pan with 10 paper bake cups. Pile ice cream mixture into cups. Freeze till firm. Makes 10 servings.

SHERBET AND SPICE

1 pint lemon sherbet
1 tablespoon finely chopped
　candied ginger

Stir sherbet just to soften. Fold in ginger. Turn into chilled refrigerator tray. Freeze till firm. Serve with fresh fruit for dessert.

HONG KONG SUNDAES

- 1 11-ounce can mandarin oranges
- 1 tablespoon cornstarch
- 1 8¾-ounce can (1 cup) crushed pineapple
- ½ cup orange marmalade
- ½ teaspoon ground ginger
  • • •
- ½ cup sliced preserved kumquats

Drain mandarin oranges, reserving ¼ cup syrup. In saucepan, blend reserved syrup and cornstarch. Stir in undrained pineapple, the marmalade, and ginger. Cook and stir over medium heat till mixture thickens and bubbles. Stir in mandarin oranges and kumquats. Serve warm or cold over vanilla ice cream. Makes 2½ cups sauce.

TROPICAL FRUIT TOPPER

- 1 cup finely chopped dates
- 1 cup water
- ½ cup finely chopped figs
- ½ cup light corn syrup
- ½ cup coarsely chopped pecans

Combine dates, water, figs, and corn syrup in small saucepan. Cook and stir over low heat till mixture thickens, 15 minutes. Remove from heat; stir in pecans. Serve warm or cool over vanilla ice cream. Makes 1⅓ cups sauce.

PEANUT MALLOW SAUCE

For final touch top with toasted coconut—

Melt one 5½-ounce package (1 cup) peanut butter pieces in ½ cup light cream over low heat, stirring constantly. Add ½ cup miniature marshmallows, continuing to stir till melted. Remove from heat; add 1 teaspoon vanilla. Serve warm or cold on ice cream. Makes 1½ cups sauce.

Sundae with Oriental flair

← Hong Kong Sundaes are a concoction of pineapple, mandarin oranges, kumquats, and marmalade with a jazz of ginger.

PEACH PECAN MOLD

- 1 quart vanilla ice cream
- 2 teaspoons rum flavoring
- ½ cup chopped pecans
  Pecan halves
  Peach Sauce

Stir ice cream to soften slightly. Blend in flavoring and chopped pecans. Arrange a few pecan halves in top of 4-cup mold. Add ice cream mixture; freeze till firm, 6 hours or overnight. To unmold, invert on serving plate and press hot damp towel closely around mold till ice cream loosens. If desired, garnish with pressurized dessert topping and thawed frozen sliced peaches. Serve with Peach Sauce.

Peach Sauce: Stir one 12-ounce can (1½ cups) peach nectar into 1 tablespoon cornstarch in small saucepan. Add ¼ cup light corn syrup. Cook and stir till boiling; cook 2 minutes longer. Stir in 1 tablespoon butter, 1 tablespoon lemon juice, and dash ground mace; cool. Just before serving, add one 12-ounce package frozen peaches, thawed, drained, and coarsely chopped. Serves 6 to 8.

PHONY SPUMONI

- 1 2-ounce package dessert topping mix
- ⅓ cup quartered red and green maraschino cherries
- 1 tablespoon chopped candied orange peel
- 1 tablespoon chopped almonds, toasted
  • • •
- 1 quart vanilla ice cream

Prepare dessert topping mix according to package directions. Fold in cherries, orange peel, and almonds; set aside. Stir ice cream to soften slightly. Press on bottom and sides of 6-cup mold or foil-lined 8½x4½x2½-inch loaf dish, forming uniform shell. Working quickly, spoon dessert topping mixture into center of mold. (If ice cream becomes too soft while forming shell in mold, place mold in freezer long enough to set ice cream before adding dessert topping center.) Freeze 6 to 8 hours or overnight. Unmold. Garnish with a piping of pressurized dessert topping. Serves 6 to 8.

ALMOND FUDGE DELIGHT

Whip ½ cup whipping cream with 1 tablespoon sugar and ¼ teaspoon rum flavoring in small bowl; fold in 1 cup milk-chocolate fudge topping. Serve on ice cream; top with toasted sliced almonds. Makes 2 cups sauce.

STRAWBERRY BANANA SHAKE

- 1 10-ounce package frozen strawberries, thawed
- 2 or 3 ripe medium bananas, sliced
- ¼ cup sugar
- 1 quart cold milk
- ¼ teaspoon almond extract
  Few drops red food coloring

Combine ingredients in blender. Blend till smooth and foamy. Serve icy cold. Serves 6.

CHERRY SPARKLE

This pastel pink soda is party pretty—

- 1 ½-ounce envelope unsweetened cherry-flavored soft drink powder
- 1 cup sugar
- 2 cups milk
- 1 quart vanilla ice cream
- 1 quart carbonated water

Combine soft drink powder and sugar. Dissolve in milk. Pour into 6 to 8 soda glasses. Add scoops of ice cream and carefully pour in the carbonated water. Stir to muddle slightly. Makes 6 to 8 servings.

APRICOT SHAKE

- 1 1-pound 5-ounce can apricot pie filling
- 1 quart vanilla ice cream
- 2 cups milk*
- 1 tablespoon lemon juice

Place pie filling, ice cream, milk, and lemon juice in mixer bowl (to use electric blender, divide recipe for two batches); blend well. Pour into 4 or 5 chilled tall glasses.

*For thinner shake, add ¼ cup more milk.

FRUITED TANGERINE ICE

- 2 7-ounce bottles ginger ale
- 1 6-ounce can frozen tangerine juice concentrate
- 1 1-pound 14-ounce can fruit cocktail, chilled and drained

Combine ginger ale and tangerine concentrate; stir just till concentrate melts. Pour into refrigerator tray; freeze till firm. At serving time, break into chunks; beat with electric or rotary beater just till broken up (don't overbeat). Stir in fruit cocktail and serve in chilled glasses. Serves 6 to 8.

STRAWBERRY FROSTED SODA

- 1 cup boiling water
- 1 3-ounce package strawberry-flavored gelatin
- 1 quart cold milk
- 1 quart strawberry ice cream

Place boiling water and gelatin in blender container; cover and blend till gelatin is dissolved. Pour ½ *cup* of the gelatin mixture into a measuring cup; set aside. Add *half* the milk to remaining gelatin mixture in blender container; blend on low speed till well-mixed. Add *half* the ice cream; cover and blend just till smooth. Pour into tall glasses. Repeat with reserved gelatin mixture, milk, and ice cream. Garnish each glass with a fresh strawberry, if desired. Makes 6 servings.

TANGY CITRUS FIZZ

- ¾ cup cold orange juice
- 1 cup vanilla ice cream
- ½ cup lemon sherbet
- 1 teaspoon aromatic bitters
- 1 7-ounce bottle lemon-lime carbonated beverage

In electric mixer bowl or blender container, combine orange juice, vanilla ice cream, lemon sherbet, and bitters. Beat or blend till smooth. Pour into 2 tall glasses. Carefully pour in carbonated beverage. Stir gently. Garnish each serving with a twist of lime, if desired. Makes 2 servings.

INDEX

Pages of this final section are for adding recipes from future issues of Better Homes and Gardens magazine and other favorite jiffy recipes.